Coffee Breaks of Faith

Coffee Breaks of Faith

Marjorie L. Kimbrough

DIMENSIONS
FOR LIVING
NASHVILLE

COFFEE BREAKS OF FAITH

Copyright © 2002 by Dimensions for Living

All rights reserved.
No part of this work may be reproduced or transmitted in any form or by any means, electronic or mechanical, including photocopying and recording, or by any information storage or retrieval system, except as may be expressly permitted by the 1976 Copyright Act or in writing from the publisher. Requests for permission should be addressed to Abingdon Press, P.O. Box 801, 201 Eighth Avenue South, Nashville, TN 37202-0801.

This book is printed on elemental-chlorine–free paper.

Library of Congress Cataloging-in-Publication Data

Kimbrough, Marjorie L., 1937-
 Coffee breaks of faith / Marjorie L. Kimbrough.
   p. cm.
 ISBN 0-687-09778-9 (bdg. pbk. : alk. paper)
 1. Bible—Meditations. 2. Christian life—Meditations. I. Title.
 BS491.5 .K56 2002
 242'.5—dc21

2002007067

All scripture quotations unless noted otherwise are taken from the *New Revised Standard Version of the Bible*, copyright 1989, by the Division of Christian Education of the National Council of the Churches of Christ in the United States of America. Used by permission. All rights reserved.

Scripture quotations noted KJV are from the King James or Authorized Version of the Bible.

02 03 04 05 06 07 08 09 10 11—10 9 8 7 6 5 4 3 2 1

MANUFACTURED IN THE UNITED STATES OF AMERICA

To

my son, Dr. Walter Mark Kimbrough, who I pray will remember to take many breaks of faith as he journeys to that college presidency

Introduction

There are times during the day when we need to be refreshed and renewed. We need a break—a coffee break of faith. We need to sit down with a cup of coffee and reflect on our faith and the faith that others have exhibited throughout history. There are historical and biblical characters whose experiences can refresh and renew us as we make our own journeys through life.

This book of meditations is designed to be used during those breaks. Read them slowly; reflect on their meaning; ask yourself what lesson they reveal in and for your life. I have chosen scriptures and stories from each book of the Bible. There are several meditations from some of the books and at least one from every book. Although I quote just one key verse from the scripture, if it is convenient, read the entire passage. Keep this book in a place that is easily accessible, and refer to it often.

Relax! We are taking coffee breaks of faith!

YIELD NOT TO TEMPTATION

GENESIS 39

She caught hold of his garment, saying, "Lie with me!" But he left his garment in her hand, and fled and ran outside. (Genesis 39:12)

❧

Joseph found himself in a position of power and trust. Even though his jealous brothers had sold him into slavery, he had been appointed overseer of Potiphar's house and was in charge of everything. Potiphar never worried about Joseph or his possessions, for it was clear that the Lord blessed all that Joseph did.

Joseph's being powerful, blessed of the Lord, and handsome was more than Potiphar's wife could resist. She was persistent in trying to seduce Joseph, but he explained that she was the only thing that had been kept from him and that he would not violate that trust. Angry from rejection, Potiphar's wife framed Joseph, and he was imprisoned. Even in jail, he prospered, for the Lord was with him. He did not yield to temptation.

Our present-day leaders could learn much from Joseph's integrity. Given charge over some things, they often take so much more. Sometimes it is taking advantage of a young employee, and sometimes it is skimming a little money off the top of a transaction. Somehow these are temptations that they cannot resist.

What temptations lure you today? Are you considering borrowing a few office supplies? Is there an affair in your future? Do you want to use foul language to express your anger? Is the escape that drugs offer appealing to you? Whatever the temptation, remember Joseph's ability not to yield. You can do it too, and God will bless you.

Lord, there are times when I just want to yield to the temptations around me. Give me the strength and courage to resist. I know you will bless me just as you blessed Joseph. Amen.

Finding a Way

Exodus 1–2:10

When she could hide him no longer she got a papyrus basket for him, and plastered it with bitumen and pitch; she put the child in it and placed it among the reeds on the bank of the river.
(Exodus 2:3)

❦

Jochebed, Moses' mother, had to find a way to save her baby. She knew that an order had been issued to kill all male babies born to Hebrew women. She also knew that midwives were refusing to kill male babies at birth, so Pharaoh had ordered them thrown into the Nile.

Jochebed hid her baby for as long as she could. Then she made a basket for him and trusted God to keep him alive. She knew the real meaning of the expression, "Find a way or make one."

How often do we face obstacles and simply throw

in the towel? We see no way out, so we give up. What is it that you are facing today that seems to be more than you can deal with? Is your boss getting on your last nerve? Is your spouse abusive? Are your children belligerent? Or are you just sick and tired?

Jochebed found a way. She engaged in creative action that saved her baby. God had a plan for that baby, and Jochebed participated in that plan by making a way. God did not love her any more than he loves us. And if God helped her make a way, so will he help us. Ask him to help you!

Lord, there are times when I just cannot go on. I feel as though there is no way out for me. I know my situation is not impossible, for all things are possible with you. Give me the creative vision I need to help me find a way or make one. Amen.

KEEPING THE SABBATH

LEVITICUS 23

Six days shall work be done; but the seventh day is a sabbath of complete rest, a holy convocation; you shall do no work: it is a sabbath to the LORD throughout your settlements. (Leviticus 23:3)

As the Lord continues to give Moses instructions for the people delivered from bondage, he calls for observing a day of complete rest and devotion to him alone. If God could create the heavens and the earth in six days, surely his people could complete their minor tasks in six days. If God needed a day of rest and reflection, so did his people.

Whether we observe the Jewish Sabbath from sundown on Friday until sundown on Saturday or the Lord's Day on Sunday, the day of the resurrection, we simply must observe one day devoted to rest and worship.

How many times do we treat the Sabbath as just another day of work? We even put off some household chores until Sunday. Often we are too tired to go to church or even to spend time in prayer and meditation. If we continue to ignore the instructions that God gave to Moses, how long will God continue to bless us?

God has been so good to us, and he deserves honor, praise, adoration, and worship. We need to spend time in quiet reflection on the blessing of the previous six days. We need to send up songs of thanksgiving and hymns of praise.

Even now, decide to take time to be holy. God has commanded it, and we must be obedient.

Lord, I promise to be more faithful in my observance of the Sabbath as a day of rest and devotion to you. Amen.

THE PRIESTLY BENEDICTION

NUMBERS 6:22-27

The Lord bless you and keep you. (Numbers 6:24)

❧

Aaron and his sons were priests, and God gave Moses the priests' blessing that should be used for the people of Israel. Moses was instructed to give this blessing to the priests. It is a wonderful benediction, and I am moved every time I hear it.

There is beautiful music set to the words of this priestly benediction, and choirs all over the world sing it with power and adoration. My high school's a cappella choir always sang this benediction to the graduates as they left campus on graduation night. What a wonderful way to go out into the world!

Just think of what this blessing promises. The Lord will bless and keep us. The Lord will look favorably and graciously upon us and will grant us peace. What more could one want? Surely if we have God's blessing, safekeeping, favor, and grace, we will live in peace.

The benediction was given to the priests to bestow upon the people—God's people. But we all are priests as members of the priesthood of believers. Let us begin to extend this benediction to each other as we part company. Perhaps some of us would live better lives knowing that God is blessing and keeping us as we go.

Lord, I need your blessing and keeping. Please make your face to shine upon me and grant me peace. Amen.

KEEPING THE GREAT COMMANDMENT

DEUTERONOMY 6

Keep these words that I am commanding you today in your heart. (Deuteronomy 6:6)

❧

After Moses had given the Israelites the Ten Commandments, he gave them the Great Commandment. It was, "You shall love the LORD your God with all your heart, and with all your soul, and with all your might" (6:5). The people were told to love God alone and to keep this commandment in their hearts. They were to recite these words to their children and talk about the commandment in their homes and away from their homes. They were to write these words on their doorposts and recite them upon rising and lying down. This Great Commandment from God was to rule their lives.

❧

Moses gave the people what God had given him. He knew that if they really loved God alone and put their hearts, souls, and might into that loving, they would obey the other commandments as well. It was just that simple. Those who really love God find it easy to be obedient to his direction.

Moses also knew that the only way the people could keep this commandment was to know it. They had to internalize it, make it a part of their daily life, teach it to their children, and make it visible in their homes.

As I review the instructions Moses gave to the Israelites, I cannot help wondering what words we keep in our hearts. What commandment do we talk to our children about? What is on our lips when we rise and when we lie down? What kinds of images and words are visible in our homes? What would Moses think of us as followers of the Great Commandment?

Let us resolve to commit the Great Commandment to memory, to keep it in our hearts, and to obey it in our lives. What a wonderful world we would experience if we only would submit to the Great Commandment!

Lord, we, like the Israelites, have failed to keep the Great Commandment. Forgive us, and strengthen us to repent and become the obedient servants we were intended to be. Amen.

STAYING ON TARGET

JOSHUA 1

Only be strong and very courageous, being careful to act in accordance with all the law that my servant Moses commanded you; do not turn from it to the right hand or to the left, so that you may be successful wherever you go. (Joshua 1:7)

Moses was dead. He had led the people as far as God had allowed. Now it was Joshua's turn to lead. God gave him very specific instructions. He was to take the Israelites across the Jordan to the land that had been promised. No enemy would ever overtake them, and all the land from the wilderness to the Great Sea would be theirs.

God promised Joshua that he would be with him even as he had been with Moses, but Joshua had to be strong. He had to know the law, and he could not stray to the right or to the left of it. He had to stay on target, and he had to keep the people on target. That was the only way they could be successful.

I wonder how many times we have failed to stay on task, on target. How easy it is to become distracted by lesser things. We have important assignments to finish, but we stop to hold a frivolous conversation. We have household chores to complete, but we stop to watch television. Sometimes we just do not stay on target.

What if God gave us Joshua's instructions? What if we knew that all we had to do was be strong and courageous and keep the law and success was guaranteed? Could we do it? How many times do we improvise the law? We move it to the right and to the left, depending on our needs. We make the law fit us; we do not conform to the law.

We, like Joshua, must stay on target to achieve our goals. God has promised success. All we have to do is be obedient.

Father God, we often fail because we move from the target you set before us. Give us strength and courage to stay the course. Amen.

LED BY A WOMAN

JUDGES 4

Barak said to her, "If you will go with me, I will go; but if you will not go with me, I will not go." (Judges 4:8)

The Israelites were sold into the hand of the Canaanite king because they had provoked God to anger with their evil deeds. They had been oppressed by the Canaanites for twenty years, and when they cried out to God for deliverance, God answered through Deborah, a prophetess and judge. Although God had sent judges before Deborah to lead Israel back to obedience, they had not ceased to worship other gods. So Israel was in trouble, suffering Canaanite oppression.

But Deborah was not only a judge who calmly

advised the people while sitting under a palm tree, but also a prophetess. God spoke to her, and she in turn was able to speak to the people. She sent for the Israelite captain, Barak, and told him to take his position while she drew out Sisera, the Canaanite general.

But Barak refused to go without Deborah. Although she agreed to go with him, she let him know that he would receive no glory from the victory; a woman was to be glorified. Barak had to accept that he was afraid to go into battle without Deborah and that a woman was to gain the victory.

How many men would have followed a woman into battle? How many would have allowed a woman to be credited with victory? Barak did. And the woman who led him was not the woman who gained the victory. Deborah knew that the woman God had chosen was Jael, the woman who would lure Sisera into her tent and kill him.

Women are strong leaders, and it is necessary to follow them when God commands it. What strong, God-fearing woman would you follow today?

Lord, you send us leaders of both genders. Help us recognize and appreciate your leaders wherever we find them. Amen.

THE BLESSING OF BEING NOTICED

RUTH 2

Then Boaz said to his servant who was in charge of the reapers, "To whom does this young woman belong?" (Ruth 2:5)

❦

Ruth had asked for permission to go into the fields to glean and perhaps find favor with someone who would provide for her mother-in-law, Naomi, and herself. Being granted that permission, Ruth went to the fields and worked hard all day without taking a break. Her beauty and hard work paid off, for Boaz noticed her.

Now Boaz was a wealthy man and a relative of Naomi's. He made instant provisions for Ruth to glean only in his fields, and he ordered the young men not to bother her. Boaz had noticed her and wanted her. He was willing to make provisions for her and Naomi.

❦

What if Ruth had not been serious about working hard? What if she had just stood around all day hoping to be noticed? Would Boaz have inquired about her? He probably would not. Although there may have been many beautiful women around the fields, there were not that many who worked hard all day without taking a break.

We never know who is noticing us. On our jobs, there may be coworkers watching. In our homes, our spouses and children may be watching. In our communities, our neighbors may be watching. In our churches, other Christians are watching, and everywhere, God is watching. What do they see? Are they watching a lazy person half doing his or her job? Or do they see a person committed to doing the very best?

Ruth was noticed, and she was rewarded. Boaz became her husband, and they became the great-grandparents of King David. What a blessing it is to be noticed for working hard!

Lord, keep me mindful that others are noticing and may be influenced by my actions. I want them to be inspired by what they see. Amen.

Provoked to Action

1 Samuel 1

Her rival used to provoke her severely, to irritate her, because the LORD had closed her womb.
(1 Samuel 1:6)

Elkanah had two wives. There was Hannah, whom he dearly loved, and Peninnah, who had borne him several children. Because Elkanah loved Hannah more than he loved Peninnah, he was more generous in his sacrificial offerings to her. This angered Peninnah. After all, she was the one who had borne him children. In retaliation, Peninnah provoked Hannah severely year after year.

Hannah was tired of being provoked, and she knew that the only way she could get Peninnah to stop was to have children of her own. She wanted children, but her womb was closed. She knew that God was the only one who could open her womb, so she prayed to him with great fervor. In fact, she prayed so fervently that Eli, the priest, thought that she was drunk. She convinced Eli that she was not drunk and solicited his help in praying that God would grant her request.

Hannah had been provoked to action. She accepted the provocation and turned it into a challenging request of and promise to God. If God would grant her a male child, she would dedicate that child's life to him.

What provokes you? Are you simply provoked or do you turn that provocation into positive action? If you are upset about something, think of the positive actions that will relieve you. Is it within your power to change, or do you, like Hannah, need the help of God and the saints?

Hannah's petition was granted, and she kept her promise to God. She was faithful. Are you?

Lord, give me the faith of Hannah to respond positively to provocation. Amen.

ACT OF KINDNESS

2 SAMUEL 4:4, 9

David asked, "Is there still anyone left of the house of Saul to whom I may show kindness for Jonathan's sake?" (2 Samuel 9:1)

❧

King Saul and his son, Jonathan, were dead. David was the new king. Although near the end of his reign, Saul had tried to kill David, David remembered his beloved friend Jonathan and wanted to show kindness to anyone related to him. It did not matter that Saul had been evil; Jonathan had been good, and his goodness needed to be rewarded.

Jonathan did have a son who was still alive. His name was Mephibosheth, and he was lame. A nurse had dropped him as she fled from the enemy. When

Mephibosheth's identity was made known, David sent for him and told him that he would always be welcome at his table as one of his sons. In addition, David instructed his servants to give all of the land that had belonged to Saul to his grandson, Mephibosheth. The land was to be tilled and its produce brought to Mephibosheth.

Mephibosheth did not feel worthy of this act of kindness, but David did not do it for him. He did it for Jonathan. Jonathan's son deserved to be provided for. He was the grandson of the first king of Israel. David respected his ancestry.

Do we ever do acts of kindness for the sake of others? Is there someone that you can honor by showing kindness to others? Although good and kind acts do not make us good, good people do good and kind acts. David was a good person. So was Jonathan, and Mephibosheth benefited. Who will benefit from the acts of kindness you will show because of the goodness of others?

Lord, give us a generous spirit that will allow us to show acts of kindness just because we are striving to be good people. Amen.

Jumping the Gun

1 Kings 1–2

Now Adonijah son of Haggith exalted himself, saying, "I will be king"; he prepared for himself chariots and horsemen, and fifty men to run before him. (1 Kings 1:5)

Adonijah was David's fourth son. He was born after Absalom and was very handsome. Since Absalom was dead, Adonijah figured that he was next in line for the throne. So he decided to exalt himself. He conferred with one of the priests and his cousin, Joab, made sacrifices, and invited all of his brothers except Solomon and declared himself king. He did all of this without the knowledge of his father David who was quite old.

The prophet Nathan told Bathsheba, Solomon's mother, that Adonijah had become king and reminded her that David had promised Solomon would succeed him as king. Supported by Nathan, Bathsheba went to David and reminded him of his promise. David proceeded to have Solomon anointed king over Israel.

When Adonijah and the friends who had gathered to celebrate his becoming king heard what had happened, they were afraid that Solomon would kill them. Adonijah's friends deserted him, and he was left alone to beg Solomon for his life. He had jumped the gun in exalting himself. He had not even informed his father that he planned to succeed him.

How often do we jump the gun? Sometimes we are so impatient for changes in our life that we assume positions that are not rightfully ours. We must learn to wait to be exalted; we must not exalt ourselves; we don't want to be asked to step down. This admonition is still good, "Wait to be asked; don't proceed on your own."

Lord, give us the patience to wait. We are often anxious to move to the next position when we have not yet finished the position where we are. If we are to be exalted, you will do that. We do not need to exalt ourselves. Amen.

A God Who Never Sleeps

1 Kings 18

At noon Elijah mocked them, saying. "Cry aloud! Surely he is a god; either he is meditating, or he has wandered away, or he is on a journey, or perhaps he is asleep and must be awakened."
(1 Kings 18:27)

Elijah challenged the people of Israel to choose the god whom they would serve. He said, "How long will you go limping with two different opinions? If the LORD is God, follow him; but if Baal, then follow him" (18:21). The people did not answer his challenge, so he explained that he was the only one of the Lord's prophets left while there were 450 prophets of Baal. Then he asked for a test to prove who was really the God who should be served. Two bulls were to be prepared for sacrifice, but no fire was to be provided. Baal's prophets would pray that their god would provide the fire for their bull, and Elijah would pray for the Lord God to provide the fire. The god that provided the fire would be the true God.

Baal's prophets went first, and after praying from morning until noon without success, Elijah told them to cry louder. He assumed their god was asleep or was not paying attention to them. By midday, Baal's prophets were so frustrated that they cut themselves with swords and lances until the blood gushed out over them. Still, there was no response from their sleeping god.

Knowing that Baal had been defeated, Elijah told the people to pour water over his bull, not once but three times. Then he prayed to God to send the fire, proving that he was the God over all Israel. God was not asleep and answered by sending a fire so powerful that it consumed the offering, the stones, and the dust. It even licked up the water that had run into the trenches.

Isn't it wonderful to serve a God who never sleeps and is always paying attention to our every need? What can you do today to show your gratitude?

Lord, thank you for not going to sleep on the job. Sometimes we do, but we are so grateful that you do not. Amen.

CONFIDENT OF THE OUTCOME

2 KINGS 4:8-37

Run at once to meet her, and say to her, Are you all right? Is your husband all right? Is the child all right? She answered, "It is all right." (2 Kings 4:26)

❧

The Shunammite woman had been kind to Elisha. She had convinced her husband to prepare a room for him so that he would have a place to stay whenever he came their way. Elisha was so appreciative that he wanted to do something for the woman. After conferring with his servant, he decided that the one thing missing from her life was a child. Elisha told her that she would have a child, and it was so.

One day the child became ill and died. The Shunammite woman did not tell her husband that the child was dead; she simply laid the child in Elisha's room and had a donkey brought to her so that she could go quickly to find Elisha. When her husband asked her why she was going to see Elisha, she answered, "It will be all right." She was confident that once she got to the man of God, everything would be all right. This man who had a double share of Elijah's spirit could raise her child from the dead.

When she reached Elisha and was asked by his servant if everyone was all right, she changed her response. She no longer said, "It *will be* all right." Seeing the man of God, she said, "It *is* all right." She knew that by the power of God, Elisha could and would make it all right.

Have you ever needed that kind of confidence in an outcome? Is there an illness or a job or a test that you are unsure of? What man or woman of God do you need to see to know that it will be all right? Is it possible to have the kind of faith that the Shunammite woman had?

Jesus told us that all we need is faith the size of a grain of mustard seed. And we can move mountains. The Shunammite woman knew that her faith in Elisha's connection to God would move the mountain of death. What about you?

Lord, give us that mountain-moving faith. Amen.

MINISTERED TO BY MUSIC

1 CHRONICLES 6:31-48

They ministered with song before the tabernacle of the tent of meeting, until Solomon had built the house of the LORD in Jerusalem; and they performed their service in due order.
(1 Chronicles 6:32)

❦

After the ark of the Lord came to rest in the place where the temple of the Lord would be built, David appointed musicians to be in charge of the service of song. David knew of the soothing power of music, for he remembered having been asked to play his harp to soothe Saul when evil spirits were tormenting him. He wanted those who would build the house of the Lord to experience that soothing power.

Although David did not know it at the time, he was not to build the temple. But by appointing those responsible for the service of song, David was providing the calm atmosphere his son Solomon would need as the tedious work of building the temple progressed. He wanted the music to minister to the workers. That music would minister to his son, too.

Have you ever been ministered to by music? Have you experienced the calm that music provides or the exuberance that it can instill? Music is a powerful tool of worship. Think of a time when a song lifted your spirits. Where were you, and what were you doing? Do you need that feeling now? If you do, start to hum or sing your favorite hymn. That's what David did, and his spirit was renewed.

What musicians have been appointed to provide the service of song where you worship? If they do not minister to your spirit, ask for new appointments. This ministry is too powerful to be ignored.

Lord, bless the musicians who minister to us. Increase their skills so that your presence can be felt in their service of song. Amen.

Seeking the Wrong Counsel

1 Chronicles 10

So Saul died for his unfaithfulness; he was unfaithful to the Lord in that he did not keep the command of the Lord; moreover, he had consulted a medium, seeking guidance. (1 Chronicles 10:13)

❧

Saul had been chosen king over Israel. He stood head and shoulders above the crowd, but he never really became the Lord's committed servant. Evil spirits sometimes possessed him, and he became jealous of David's great ability as a warrior. He was unfaithful in keeping the command of the Lord. He even sought counsel from a medium rather than from God.

Saul's unfaithfulness led to his death, and it was a horrible death. He deliberately fell on his own sword and was later beheaded, and his body was fastened to the wall of Bethshan. It took some valiant men who traveled all night to take his body off the wall and bury his bones. It is obvious that these men were Saul's friends, for they would not leave him fastened to the wall. They respected his having been king, and they remembered the times that he had served God.

What happened to Saul? Why, after all he had accomplished, did he turn from God and seek the counsel of a medium? Had the medium anointed him king over Israel? Had the medium helped him defeat the enemy? Had the medium blessed his household and given him sons? Did the medium advise him to take his own life?

What happens to us when we seek the counsel of astrologers and fortune-tellers? Have they blessed us as God has? Do we trust them more than we trust God? Do we know valiant men who will travel all night to take our bodies off the wall and bury our bones?

God is faithful, and we must be faithful to him, for only he is able to deliver us.

Lord, I need your guidance. You alone can help me keep your commandments and live a life that is faithful to you. Amen.

STICK WITH GOD

2 CHRONICLES 14–15

He went out to meet Asa and said to him, "Hear me, Asa, and all Judah and Benjamin: The LORD is with you, while you are with him. If you seek him, he will be found by you, but if you abandon him, he will abandon you." (2 Chronicles 15:2)

When Asa, the great-grandson of Solomon, assumed the throne, he removed all foreign altars and commanded that the people seek God. He reminded the people of Judah that God had delivered their ancestors and had given them land and wealth. The people followed Asa's advice, and God granted them peace for many years.

The peace was interrupted when the Ethiopians came with an army of a million men and three hundred chariots against Asa's army of five hundred eighty thousand carrying shields, spears, and bows.

Asa prayed for God's deliverance, and God defeated the Ethiopians. After capturing all of the cities around Gerar, Asa and his army returned to Jerusalem.

Upon his return, Asa was given some priestly advice. He was told that the Lord would be with him as long as he was with the Lord. God would always answer him and would not abandon him. He was advised to be courageous, for God would reward his work.

Asa followed this advice, removed idols from the land, and led the people in sacrificing to God and in affirming a covenant to seek the Lord with all their heart and soul. They sealed their covenant with an oath in loud voices. All who refused to take the oath to stick with God were put to death.

I wonder how willing we are to stick with God. Would we take an oath promising to seek him with all our heart and soul? Would we be motivated by the threat of death? The advice Asa received reminds us that God does not abandon us; we abandon him. Stick with God!

Lord, we often let idols distract us, but we know that only you are faithful to us. Make us faithful to you. Amen.

A Stirred Up Spirit

Ezra 1

The heads of the families of Judah and Benjamin, and the priests and the Levites—everyone whose spirit God had stirred—got ready to go up and rebuild the house of the LORD in Jerusalem. (Ezra 1:5)

❧

King Cyrus was the first to be stirred up at the end of the Babylonian captivity. The spirit of God so moved on him that he announced to all who claimed to be the people of God that they were permitted to go to Jerusalem and rebuild God's temple. Everyone whose spirit God had stirred went to Jerusalem.

God's people did not go alone. They took with them silver, gold, goods, animals, and offerings for the house of God. King Cyrus even returned the sacred vessels that Nebuchadnezzar had taken and placed in the house of his gods. They were stirred up for God.

Have you ever felt the hand of God compelling you to get up and do something? Have you ever felt stirred up? The people of Israel did, and they accomplished great things. They had a leader who was stirred up, and he, in turn, with God's help, was able to stir them up.

What would it take to stir us up? Would it be a call to rebuild a church that had been destroyed? Would it be a drive to feed and clothe the hungry? Would it be the cry for a court-appointed advocate for child prostitutes? Would it be the millions suffering from dreaded diseases? What would it take?

God calls us to get stirred up. There is so much to be done to bring about his kingdom, and he needs some workers in the world. He has enough temples. Recognize his spirit stirring within you. Get stirred up!

Father, we confess that we have not responded to the stirring of your spirit within us. Give us repentance. Amen.

Dealing with Oppression

Nehemiah 5

So I said, "The thing that you are doing is not good. Should you not walk in the fear of our God, to prevent the taunts of the nations our enemies!"
(Nehemiah 5:9)

❧

Nehemiah discovered that some Jewish people were being sold by kin. Some had to pledge their fields and houses in order to feed their families, and they had to borrow to pay taxes. Nehemiah was so angry that he brought charges against the nobles and officials. He told them that they were taking interest from their own people. He reminded them that they had always bought back their own Jewish kindred who had been sold to other nations, and they were selling their own who must be bought back by their own.

❧

Nehemiah called their hand. He told them that they were wrong, and he told them to stop. He instructed them to stop charging interest, to restore their property, and to give them food. The nobles and officials promised to do what Nehemiah had asked, and Nehemiah made them take an oath to do as they had promised. He shook out the fold of his garment and said, "So may God shake out everyone from house and from property who does not perform this promise. Thus may they be shaken out and emptied" (5:13).

Nehemiah was bold and courageous in his opposition to oppression. What about us? If we find someone who is being cheated, overtaxed, having his or her property taken, or being deprived of food, do we deal with it or just ignore it? There are so many instances of oppression like this in our world. If we each would decide to deal with just one instance, what a difference it would make.

God needs some Nehemiahs today. Will you speak up for someone today? Will you back up your words with an affirmation that God is able to shake out and empty anyone who continues to oppress? Will you be a Nehemiah?

Lord, give me Nehemiah's courage to speak out against oppression. Amen.

BEING IN THE RIGHT PLACE AT THE RIGHT TIME

ESTHER 4

For if you keep silence at such a time as this, relief and deliverance will rise for the Jews from another quarter, but you and your father's family will perish. Who knows? Perhaps you have come to royal dignity for just such a time as this. (Esther 4:14)

❦

Esther had been chosen to replace Vashti as queen. The fact that she was a Jew was not known. So when the king's top official, Haman, set out to kill all Jews because Mordecai, Esther's cousin, refused to bow down to him, Mordecai sent word to Esther. He begged her to go before the king and reveal Haman's plan. Esther let Mordecai know that it had been thirty days since the king had sent for her, and if anyone went to the king without having been summoned, that person would die unless the king extended the golden scepter.

❦

Although Mordecai understood Esther's reluctance to go before the king, he reminded her that she would not be spared just because she lived in the king's palace. If she did not act, she and her family would die, but God would find another way to relieve and deliver the Jews. She was urged to consider whether she had risen to her place of royal dignity for just such a time. After a three-day fast, Esther responded to Mordecai's request, for she was in the right place at the right time. And the Jews were spared.

In modern times, brave Christians have put their lives on the line. They, like Esther, have said that if they perish, they perish. The leaders of the Civil Rights movement often faced death in attempts to restore dignity to their people. Women have put their lives on the line for the right to vote and for the right to choose what is best for their bodies. When we find ourselves in the right place at the right time, do we rise to the challenge, or do we keep silent? Remember that Mordecai warned Esther that silence would not save her. It will not save us either. Act in faith!

Father, give us the courage to rise to the occasion wherever we are. Amen.

What It Means to Fear God

Job 1–2:10

There was once a man in the land of Uz whose name was Job. That man was blameless and upright, one who feared God and turned away from evil. (Job 1:1)

Job was a good man. He kept the Lord's commandments and was richly blessed. He had sons and daughters, houses and lands, and animals and servants. He gave offerings and praise to God not only for himself, but also for his children. He was afraid that his children might have sinned and cursed God in their hearts, and Job was not taking any chances.

When God lifted Job up as an example of an upright person, Satan pointed out Job's many blessings and implied that if they were taken away, Job no longer would be righteous. Knowing Job's heart, God allowed Job's blessings to be taken away.

Job lost his property and his children; yet, he worshiped God saying, "Naked I came from my mother's womb, and naked shall I return there; the Lord gave, and the LORD has taken away; blessed be the name of the LORD" (1:21).

When Job's health was attacked and he had sores all over his body, his wife told him to curse God and die. But Job called her a foolish woman and said, "Shall we receive the good at the hand of God, and not receive the bad?" (2:10).

When we truly fear God, we are equipped to receive both the good and the bad. We must always remember that God is in control and knows how much we can bear. If we are blameless and upright like Job, we can bear much. If we are weak and faithless, we can bear little. How much can you bear?

Father, you have blessed us with so much; yet, we falter when we are challenged with misfortune. Equip us to be God fearing like Job so that we too can praise you in whatever life brings. Amen.

LIKE A TREE

Psalm 1

They are like trees planted by streams of water, which yield their fruit in its season, and their leaves do not wither. In all that they do, they prosper. (Psalm 1:3)

How fitting it is for a psalm that praises those who delight in the law of the Lord to follow the book of Job. Although Job suffered greatly, he did not cease fearing God; he was like a tree planted by the water. He did yield his fruit in due season, and he was blessed with even more than he had originally.

The psalm states that those who do not follow the advice of the wicked are happy. Job did not follow the advice of his wife or his friends. His wife wanted him to curse God and die, and his friends wanted him to confess his sins. He simply held fast and said, "Though he slay me, yet will I trust in him" (Job 13:15*a* KJV). He knew that his redeemer was alive and well. Job was like a tree planted by the water; he would not be moved.

There is something about this first psalm that speaks to all of us when we are tempted to stray from God's law. The Negro spiritual singers proclaimed, "I shall not; I shall not be moved. I shall not; I shall not be moved. Just like a tree planted by the waters, I shall not be moved." As slaves, they delighted in the law of the Lord, and like Job, they knew that their redeemer was alive. No man could drag them so low as to make them hate him. They held on to their faith.

What do you need to hold on to? Are you easily moved, or do you hold to your convictions? Think about it. Consider the tree, and emulate it.

Father, make us steadfast and immovable in our faith and commitment to you. Let us be just like trees. Amen.

CROWNED WITH GLORY AND HONOR

PSALM 8

*Yet you have made them a little lower than God,
and crowned them with glory and honor.
(Psalm 8:5)*

The psalmist does some serious reflecting on the power and majesty of God and his generous gifts to humankind. God created human beings in his own image and crowned them with glory and honor. We as humans were put in charge of the earth and all its living entities. Why were we given this great glory?

God knew that we had the ability to rule his creation. After all, he created us and gave us all that was necessary to live in honor. God did not make us robots that would do only what he told us to do. He made us free to make choices. God wanted us to choose to obey him; he wanted us to earn our glory; he wanted us to live in honor. Have any of us lived up to the Creator's expectations?

Let us consider just what we, as God's human creation, have done with God's environmental creation. We waste natural resources; we fill lakes and streams with pollution; we kill endangered species. We cut down trees and waste paper. We must admit that we are not very resourceful in environmental issues.

Then what are we as God's human creation doing to ourselves? Many of us load our bodies with drugs and alcohol. Others of us abandon our children and elders. Still others of us murder our neighbors, covet what others have, do not provide for the poor, and fail to worship and serve the God of our creation.

Yet that same God continually forgives us, knows that we are able to repent and return to our original power and glory, and invites us to come to him. He even sacrificed his Son so that we might claim our crown of glory and honor. He is indeed a mighty God, majestic in all the earth!

Great Creator, help us live up to the glory and honor you intended. Amen.

Sweeter Than Honey

Psalm 19

More to be desired are they than gold, even much fine gold; sweeter also than honey, and drippings of the honeycomb. (Psalm 19:10)

Have you ever noticed how sweet honey is? What could be sweeter? Well, according to David there are six things pertaining to God that are sweeter. First is the law of the Lord, which is so perfect that it revives the soul. Second are the decrees of the Lord, which are so sure that they make the simple wise. Third are the Lord's precepts, which are so right that the heart is made to rejoice. Fourth is the Lord's clear commandment, which enlightens the eyes. Fifth is the fear of the Lord, which in its purity endures forever. And sixth are the Lord's ordinances, which are so true that they are altogether righteous.

These six—law, decrees, precepts, commandment, fear, and ordinances—are to be desired more than gold and sweeter than honey and the drippings of the honeycomb. All six imply knowledge of God and his design for our living in perfect harmony with all of his creation.

In order to proclaim with David the desirability and sweetness of the law and commandments of God, we must know and abide by them. David admitted that there is great reward in keeping the law. He prayed that he would not be influenced by the insolent, for he wanted to be blameless and innocent of great transgression. He ended this psalm with the very familiar words, "Let the words of my mouth and the meditation of my heart be acceptable to you, O LORD, my rock and my redeemer" (19:14).

Perhaps we should start with David's ending and pray that what we speak and what we feel will be acceptable to the God whom we recognize as our rock and redeemer. If we keep our words and thoughts in compliance with God's law, decrees, precepts, commandment, fear, and ordinances, we, like David, will know how desirable and sweet it is to trust and serve him.

Holy Father, the heavens declare your glory, and the firmaments proclaim your handiwork. Make us faithful to your sweet law. Amen.

A Cry for Help

Psalm 22

*My God, my God, why have you forsaken me?
Why are you so far from helping me, from the
words of my groaning? (Psalm 22:1)*

Although these words were spoken by Jesus on the cross (Matthew 27:46), they did not originate with him. In this psalm, these words are attributed to David, and they are a plea for deliverance from suffering and hostility. I know that we all can identify with such a plea. No one wants to suffer or be surrounded by hostility. However, suffering is something that all of us encounter. It just comes with living.

The way we handle the suffering that surely will come is the key to our successful living. I think we can learn from David and Jesus that we need to turn to God and plead for deliverance. Deliverance came in different forms for these two persons. David eventually triumphed over his enemies and was delivered from suffering and hostility. Jesus also triumphed, but he did so through death and resurrection. Most of us do not want to die to be delivered. We want deliverance in this life.

Think about the times you have felt forsaken. Were you forsaken by family or friends? Were you forsaken by your church or your pastor? Did you feel forsaken by God? Have you considered whether those times in your life were times that God just needed your undivided attention and had to do something to get it?

I believe that sometimes we suffer and encounter hostility so that we can devote our undivided attention to God. We need God to direct our lives; yet, we often believe that we are capable of doing the directing all by ourselves. God does not forsake us; we forsake him. Take the time to recognize his presence. He is with you and will deliver you.

Lord, let me feel your presence as I face this feeling of being forsaken. Make clear to me what I should learn from this situation. I know that you can and will deliver me. Amen.

Joy in the Morning

Psalm 30

For his anger is but for a moment; his favor is for a lifetime. Weeping may linger for the night, but joy comes with the morning. (Psalm 30:5)

❧

According to the *New Revised Standard Version of the Bible,* David wrote Psalm 30 in "thanksgiving for recovery from a grave illness." David is bold in his thanksgiving, even admitting that his very soul had been brought up from hell and restored to life. He urges us to praise God also because our suffering, which he attributes to God's anger, is but for a moment. God bestows his favor on us for a lifetime.

Have you ever been really sick and wondered why God had allowed the pain and suffering that had accompanied your sickness? I have. I recently fell face forward down a flight of concrete steps while volunteering at the county hospital. I was doing what I considered to be good work, but I suffered while doing it. I wondered why I had fallen. When my face was hurting so badly, I wondered who was fighting me and why I was suffering. But God was there. I did not break any bones, and I was only bruised and battered. The bruises reminded me that suffering only lasts a short while; joy comes in the morning.

What should happen to us when we suffer? I believe we should use the time to meditate on the goodness of God. We need to join David in thanking and praising God because we know that the suffering will pass. We need to discover what lesson God wants us to learn from our suffering and we need to discover how we are being prepared for the next experience.

While I was hospitalized in the county hospital, I discovered how people who have no insurance and no advocates are treated. I had both, but I observed those who had neither. I learned to be more compassionate, and I tried to encourage the doctors and nurses to extend the same courtesies to others that they were extending to me.

Bruises heal; suffering passes. Joy comes in the morning!

Thank you, God, for the joy that always follows weeping. Amen.

CAN YOU FLY?

PSALM 55

And I say, "O that I had wings like a dove! I would fly away and be at rest." (Psalm 55:6)

❧

The musician R. Kelly wrote a song entitled "I Believe I Can Fly." It is a motivational song that many young people started singing at their graduations. They believed they could fly and that they could touch the sky. They wanted to soar to new heights in their personal lives. But, in contrast, the psalmist wanted to fly away and be at rest.

Why do we wish for wings? Would we soar to new heights? Would we fly above the traffic and quickly reach our destinations? Would we hover above the problems we encounter and observe the outcome? Would we really want to be above and untouched by all that happens in our lives? Or is it possible that we just want a safe haven, a place of spiritual rest and renewal?

The psalmist wanted to escape the treachery of a friend. He wrote, "It is not enemies who taunt me—I could bear that; it is not adversaries who deal insolently with me—I could hide from them. But it is you, my equal, my friend, with whom I kept pleasant company; we walked in the house of God with the throng" (55:12-14). A friend's betrayal is almost more than one can bear. It is so much easier to deal with the betrayal of one's enemies. In light of this betrayal, the psalmist needed to escape. He needed a place of rest.

Like the psalmist, I would like to have the wings of a dove so that I could fly away and be at rest, but I would return, once refreshed, to deal with whatever sent me flying away in the first place. I would use my time away to pray for those friends who betrayed me, and I would pray for the personal wisdom to deal with whatever situation their treachery placed me in. I think we all need a place to which we can retreat. We need to take time to meditate and reflect on our lives and circumstances. We need to listen for God's direction and to discover his will for our lives.

Lord, grant us internal wings so that we can fly. Amen.

Joyful Noise

Psalm 100

Make a joyful noise to the LORD, all the earth.
(Psalm 100:1)

❦

$\mathscr{E}$very time I read Psalm 100, I think of all the people who want us to be quiet in the house of the Lord. They do not want noise; they want silent devotion. But what does God want? Is there a compromise between noise and silence?

Consider the biblical sister and brother, Miriam and Moses. They had very different styles of worship. Miriam believed in making a joyful noise. She wanted to lead the people in singing and dancing once they had successfully crossed the Red Sea. She "took a tambourine in her hand; and all the women went out after her with tambourines and with dancing" (Exodus 15:20b). Miriam wanted everyone to sing to the Lord. Miriam wanted to make a joyful noise.

In contrast, Moses expected the Israelites to listen quietly to his sermon of praise and thanksgiving. He appeared to be more stilted and reserved as he sang, "I will sing to the LORD, for he has triumphed gloriously; horse and rider he has thrown into the sea" (Exodus 15:1). I do not envision with Moses the tambourines and the dancing that are so vivid with Miriam.

Consider David and his wife, Michal, daughter of Saul. David leaped and danced before the Lord as the ark of the Lord was brought into the city. Michal thought that David's dancing was vulgar and disgraceful. But David told her, "It was before the LORD, who chose me in place of your father and all his household, to appoint me as prince over Israel, the people of the LORD, that I have danced before the Lord" (2 Samuel 6:21). Although Michal despised David's actions, God was pleased, and, perhaps as her punishment, Michal was barren until her death.

I believe that God appreciates praise whether silent or noisy. But as for me and my house, we will make a joyful noise!

Lord, we worship you with the gladness of singing, dancing, and thanksgiving. Amen.

Giving First to God

Proverbs 3

Honor the LORD with your substance and with the first fruits of all your produce. (Proverbs 3:9)

Why is it so hard for us to give first to God? We are asked to give only one tenth, and that should be given first. I once witnessed a demonstration during a sermon on tithing that made clear the small amount we are asked to give. The minister very dramatically gathered ten of several items. He had ten potatoes, ten cans of corn, ten apples, ten oranges, and so on. Then he distributed the items, taking one of each item and saying, "One for you, God, and nine for me." While God's pile increased slowly, the minister's pile quickly overflowed. We got the point.

God asks so little of us, and he gives so much. All we have is his; he simply has entrusted us with it. The writer of Proverbs lets us know that in honoring God with our substance and giving him the first fruits, we will be blessed. He writes, "Honor the Lord with your substance and with the first fruits of all your produce; then your barns will be filled with plenty, and your vats will be bursting with wine" (3:9-10). This promise should be incentive enough for us to give to God first.

What is it you are holding back from God? Is it something of your substance? Perhaps it is your time, your service, or your talent. Perhaps it is your money, a resource that God may need for ministry; but whatever it is, give it up. As long as your hand is held in a tight fist, you cannot lose whatever you are holding and cannot receive anything else. Trust God with all that you are and all that you have. Abundant blessings are in store!

Lord, today is the first day that I will truly honor you with my substance and my first fruits. I pray that this day marks the beginning of my lifelong commitment to tithing. Amen.

GOOD MEDICINE

PROVERBS 17

A cheerful heart is a good medicine, but a downcast spirit dries up the bones. (Proverbs 17:22)

Mrs. Brown had fallen and broken her hip. She was a good church member who always visited the sick, but the fall had made her one of the sick. She was very disappointed because she looked forward to her opportunities to spread cheer among the bedridden members of the congregation. She did not know how she would survive the months it would take before she would be up and about again.

Other church members decided to help Mrs. Brown. They remembered all that she had done for others and took turns visiting her. The funny thing was that after each visit, the visitors felt uplifted. Mrs. Brown was still spreading cheer, and her cheerful heart was good medicine for her and for those who came to visit her.

What if Mrs. Brown had allowed a downcast spirit to take over her life? According to the scripture, "a downcast spirit dries up the bones." Mrs. Brown certainly did not want dried up bones. She never would have walked again if her bones had dried up.

Whenever you are feeling down, think a happy thought, give someone a smile, tell a joke, or read a funny story. It will make you feel better, and you will be spreading joy to those around you.

We should never let a downcast spirit conquer us. We simply must resolve to wipe it away with the great joy that God gives us. What a joy it is to know that God loves us. Think of that, and smile!

Lord, give us a cheerful heart. It is all the medicine we need. Amen.

What Time Is It?

Ecclesiastes 3

For everything there is a season, and a time for every matter under heaven. (Ecclesiastes 3:1)

Is there really a time for every season? If there is, what time is it in your life? In what season are you living? I know that sometimes we feel as though we are living through rough times. Everything bad happens. Relatives and good friends, and even our plants, die. We lose our jobs; our children are belligerent; our spouses are abusive or alcoholic. It is a bad time, a season of unhappiness.

Or we might be living though a wonderful time, a season of joy and happiness. Our spouses are loving; our children are models of good behavior and academic achievement; we are promoted on our jobs. Everyone we know is in excellent health. It is a good time.

But according to Ecclesiastes 3, a different season awaits. If we are crying now, our time of laughing, singing, dancing, and shouting is just around the corner. If we are already letting the good times roll, our difficult time is pending.

Because the rough times are only temporary, let us concentrate on the good times in the season that is coming. What time do you want it to be in your life? What can you do to bring it about? Sometimes our very demeanor predicts doom. Perk up, look up, walk with determination, and smile. The good times are on their way. Be ready for them.

Lord, help me through this season, and fix my mind on the blessings to come. I look forward to the good time that you have in store. Amen.

BETTER THAN WINE

SONG OF SOLOMON 1

Let him kiss me with the kisses of his mouth! For your love is better than wine.
(Song of Solomon 1:2)

How many people long for sweet kisses and a love that is better than wine? I know so many people, both old and young, who want to meet someone who will love them. Love is such a powerful thing, and I don't know of anyone who does not love to get kisses. We even teach our babies to give us some "sugar." Babies learn that kisses are sweet and that they make the recipient feel good.

This verse from Song of Solomon implies that wine makes us feel good. Wine is said to complement food and make it taste better. It is also said to have relaxing power. It may even be a type of aphrodisiac. But love is even better than wine. How do we find such love? Is it only sexual love that is better than wine?

Let us consider the three types of love. There is of course eros, or sexual love. When couples truly love each other and live in the euphoria of daily bliss, I am sure that their love is better than wine. Who would exchange true love for wine? The wine would eventually give out, but true love lasts forever.

Then there is philia, or friendly love. We know the value of friends; sometimes they stick closer than a brother. There is no greater love than to give one's life for his or her friends. But is that love better than wine? Most people would say that it is. Again, the wine will run out or even become bitter, but true friends are friends forever.

Last, there is agape, or godlike love. This love is unconditional. Our sexual partners may cease to love us; our friends may become disappointed in us and desert us; but God loves us with an everlasting love. His love is truly better than wine.

Lord, let us love each other with agape love, for it is better than wine and sweet kisses put together. Amen.

When Will You See Him?

Isaiah 6

In the year that King Uzziah died, I saw the Lord sitting on a throne, high and lofty; and the hem of his robe filled the temple. (Isaiah 6:1)

❦

Isaiah saw God in the year that King Uzziah died. When will you see him? What will it take for you to have a vision of God? Will someone have to die? Does death reveal something about God to us? What does it take?

Or have you already seen God? What revealed him to you? Were you in worship surrounded by others, or were you alone? Did God's presence fill the space where you saw him, or was he just in one part of the space? What did God look like? Was he too awesome to describe?

Sometimes we never ask ourselves these types of questions, but I have always been fascinated with Isaiah's experience. I believe that Isaiah might never have seen God if King Uzziah had not died. Somehow Isaiah was so taken by the king that he never looked around and allowed God to reveal himself. There are even some translations that read, "In the year that king Uzziah died I saw *also* the Lord" (KJV, emphasis added). In addition to the king, Isaiah saw the Lord. I wonder if there is anything or anyone blocking our view of God. Do we also see the Lord?

Let's think about that. Is there a spouse, parent, friend, or child in whom you are so caught up that you cannot see the Lord? Is your job taking up so much of your time that there is no time left for God? Don't you realize that God is able to remove the obstacle? Remember that King Uzziah died, and then Isaiah saw the Lord.

Once Isaiah saw the Lord, he was able to respond to God's voice calling out for a prophet to the people. I wonder what mission God might have for us. We cannot respond until we see him.

Lord, help me see around, over, above, or under whatever or whoever is blocking my vision of you. I am ready to respond to your calling. Amen.

Highway to Heaven

Isaiah 35

A highway shall be there, and it shall be called the Holy Way; the unclean shall not travel on it, but it shall be for God's people; no traveler, not even fools, shall go astray. (Isaiah 35:8)

In chapter 35, Isaiah describes the return of the redeemed to Zion. It will be a wonderful time. Deserts shall blossom, and singing and rejoicing shall abound. The weak will be strengthened, the blind will see, the deaf will hear and speak, and the lame will walk. The glory of the Lord will be all around. There will be a highway there, which only the redeemed will travel.

I had not recognized the source of the gospel song "Highway to Heaven" until I revisited this scripture. The words to the song are, "It's a highway to heaven. None can walk up there but the pure in heart. It's a highway to heaven. I am walking up the King's highway." The scripture supports these words, for the highway is holy, and the unclean will not travel on it. It will be reserved for God's people.

To be able to sing the song and say that "I am walking up the King's highway" implies that one is living the holy and redeemed life. I wonder whether those who sing the song know what they are saying. They do not have to be smart to travel on this highway, for not even fools shall go astray. The only requirement is that one be a member of God's people, the redeemed.

Are you redeemed? Are you one of God's people? Do you expect to walk up the King's highway? I certainly want to. I am so glad that we will not encounter any ravenous beasts along the road; we will not need to fear; we will experience everlasting joy; and sorrow and sighing shall disappear. Remember that none but the pure in heart can walk up there. Is that who you are?

Lord, I want to walk up the King's highway. Help me be one of your redeemed. Amen.

WILLING TO WAIT

ISAIAH 40

But those who wait for the LORD shall renew their strength, they shall mount up with wings like eagles, they shall run and not be weary, they shall walk and not faint. (Isaiah 40:31)

❧

Waiting is often painful for us. We find it hard to wait to grow up. We can hardly wait until we are old enough to drive. We count the days until we graduate from high school or college. We painfully wait for that doctor's report or lab result. We even find it difficult to wait for the joyous occasions of Christmas, birthdays, and weddings.

Why is it so difficult to wait? Perhaps it is because we have not learned to wait on the Lord. But what does that mean? Are we waiting *on* the Lord or are we waiting *in* the Lord? There is a big difference. If we just wait on the Lord, time does not move any faster, our days are not any shorter, and our anticipation is not diminished. However, if we wait in the Lord, we are surrounded by his promises. We know and rejoice in the many blessings that he has already bestowed, and we believe that our waiting will make us stronger.

When we are actually in the Lord, we have all of the resources that he so generously supplies. We have strength, knowing that our strength has its source in him, and he is a mighty strong God. We have wings, knowing we can fly above whatever outcome awaits us. We know that we can run like an Olympian, never tiring because he keeps our legs moving. And we know that we can walk and not grow faint. What a mighty God we serve!

Are you willing to wait in and not just on him?

Lord, I am willing to wait. Help me change the way that I wait so that I am waiting in you, fully assured of your blessings. Amen.

A Unique Heritage

Isaiah 54

No weapon that is fashioned against you shall prosper, and you shall confute every tongue that rises against you in judgment. This is the heritage of the servants of the Lord and their vindication from me, says the Lord. (Isaiah 54:17)

☙❦

What a blessing it is to know and believe that no weapon formed against us shall prosper. But this blessing is true only for the servants of the Lord. Just what weapons can be formed against us?

A young man knew several women who formed weapons against him. They sought to trick him into marriage by claiming to be pregnant with his child. They tried to cause him to lose his job and to alienate him from his family. These weapons can be successful against those who are not servants of the Lord.

☙❦

Let's consider these weapons. Can we trick into marriage one who has developed a relationship that welcomes God as a third party? Can we force someone to support a child born out of wedlock if he practices abstinence before marriage? Can we jeopardize the job of one who is a loyal and faithful worker and consistently performs well? Can we alienate family members who genuinely love one another? I don't think so.

The scripture also promises that tongues raised against the Lord's servants will be confuted. This means that they don't have to worry about lies told about them. The truth will be disclosed, and the lying tongues shall cease.

If you are worried about weapons that are being formed against you or lies that are being told about you, consider your status as a servant of the Lord. Do you serve him? If you do, don't worry. His promised blessing is true.

Father God, make me a true and faithful servant. Amen.

BEING IN THE SPIRIT

ISAIAH 61

The spirit of the Lord GOD is upon me, because the LORD has anointed me; he has sent me to bring good news to the oppressed, to bind up the brokenhearted, to proclaim liberty to the captives, and release to the prisoners. (Isaiah 61:1)

❧

Jesus read this scripture in the synagogue at Nazareth near the beginning of his ministry. After reading it, Jesus said, "Today this scripture has been fulfilled in your hearing" (Luke 4:21*b*).

How wonderful it must have been to hear Jesus read these words and then proclaim their fulfillment. I wonder if those present felt the spirit of God. Could they see the anointing? Were the oppressed open to the good news that he brought? Did the brokenhearted, the captive, and the prisoners realize that their deliverance was at hand? I don't think so because Jesus was rejected at Nazareth. He had no honor in his hometown.

Why is it that we fail to recognize the spirit of God? Are we failing to seek it? When God's anointing is on someone, why don't we see it? Perhaps we are resistant to the good news. Perhaps we do not want to be released from our bondage. Some of us seem to enjoy being bound. The popularity of books that proclaim that although we may feel bound by our occupations, sexual orientation, physical appearance, or marital status, we can be loosed.

If we would simply accept the good news that Isaiah foretold and Jesus fulfilled, there would be no bondage. I wonder if that is what we truly want. Do we want to be filled with the spirit of God? Do we want his anointing? Perhaps that spirit and anointing would keep us from the secular activities that we enjoy so much. Do we want to be released from our oppression? Perhaps that would remove our ability to complain. Do we enjoy the role of the brokenhearted? Without crying, we could not have the sympathy of others. Do we relish in being captives and prisoners in our own homes? Maybe our condition makes us believe that we are successfully bearing our cross. Jesus fulfilled the promise. We are loosed.

Lord, help me feel the spirit, recognize the anointing, and claim the victory and freedom in Jesus. Amen.

Only a Boy

Jeremiah 1

But the LORD said to me, "Do not say, 'I am only a boy'; for you shall go to all to whom I send you, and you shall speak whatever I command you." (Jeremiah 1:7)

Jeremiah tried to use the excuse that he was too young to speak for God, but God said that excuse was unacceptable. The Almighty God had known Jeremiah before he was even conceived; that same God had appointed him as a prophet before he was born; and that same God would supply the words for the messages to be conveyed. Being "only a boy" just would not fly.

Jeremiah's statement that he was only a boy implied that God was limited in his power, that God was not powerful enough to use a boy. God could not give the words to a boy or send a boy to a nation in need of redemption. Jeremiah was wrong, and God made him fully aware of it.

We may be like Jeremiah. We may look at young people and believe that they are too young or only a girl or boy. But God is able to use whomever he wants whenever he wants and in whatever way he wants. Our only function is to be receptive to that girl or boy.

Is there a young person in your environment who is appointed by God? Have you discouraged him or her with your looks or acts of distrust? Have you failed to hear God's message in that young person? Look around. God may have appointed and anointed your child. No one is too young when God is involved.

Jeremiah learned this lesson as a boy. God told him not to be afraid. God touched his mouth and gave him words to speak and wisdom to rule. Jeremiah was appointed over nations and kingdoms. He was given power "to pluck up and to pull down, to destroy and to overthrow, to build and to plant" (1:10*b*). And he was only a boy.

Lord, make me sensitive to the young people with whom I come in contact. They may have a message from you especially for me. Amen.

Medicine for the Soul

Jeremiah 8–9

Is there no balm in Gilead? Is there no physician there? Why then has the health of my poor people not been restored? (Jeremiah 8:22)

❧

Jeremiah is mourning for the people. His spirit is down, all joy is gone, and he is heartsick. The people have been worshiping idol gods. Even after the harvest passed and the summer ended, the people were not saved. What was a prophet to do?

Jeremiah asks for a balm, a medicine, and a physician that could heal and restore his people. While Jeremiah asked the questions and sought the medicine for the soul, the Negro slave answered the questions when singing, "There is a balm in Gilead, to make the wounded whole. There is a balm in

Gilead, to heal the sin-sick soul." What Jeremiah and the people needed was a cure for sin. The people were sick with sin and needed to become whole.

The Negro spiritual offers the solution. Whenever the slaves felt discouraged and downhearted, they relied on the Holy Spirit to revive them. The Holy Spirit was the balm, or the medicine, for the soul.

Are we like Jeremiah, spending our time crying for the sins of the world, or are we busy offering the solution provided by the knowledge of Jesus and the presence of the Holy Spirit in our lives? Do we have to ask if there is a balm, or do we know about it because we have depended on it many times?

Jeremiah is the weeping prophet. He even wishes that his head could be a spring of water and that his eyes could be fountains of tears so that he could weep day and night. But weeping is not the answer. Only knowledge of God, obedience to his laws, and the presence of the Holy Spirit provide medicine for the sin-sick soul. There is balm in Gilead.

Father, I stretch my hand to thee. No other help I know. Please heal my sin-sick soul. Amen.

NEW EVERY MORNING

LAMENTATIONS 3

They are new every morning; great is your faithfulness. (Lamentations 3:23)

While Jeremiah was lamenting over the faithlessness of Israel, he rejoiced over the faithfulness of God. He says, "The steadfast love of the LORD never ceases, his mercies never come to an end; they are new every morning; great is your faithfulness" (3:22-23).

I wonder how many of us really take the time to consider the fact that God gives us new love and mercies every morning. We often remember to thank God for each new year; we even make new year's resolutions. But how many of us thank God for each new morning? Do we even consider making new day's resolutions? I think we should.

In my book *Beyond Limitations*, I suggest that as soon as we wake up in the morning, we should thank God for the day and for the opportunity to be the best person we can be that day. We should make a new day's resolution. What can I do and be for God this day? We might have better luck in keeping a new day's resolution than we do in keeping our new year's resolutions.

God is faithful to us every day, but are we faithful to God? Have we, like Israel, forgotten how good and faithful God is? Thomas O. Chisholm remembered that God is faithful every day when he penned the words to the hymn, "Great Is Thy Faithfulness" in 1923. God gives us new love and mercy every morning. Consider his words, "Great is thy faithfulness! Great is thy faithfulness! Morning by morning new mercies I see; all I have needed thy hand hath provided; great is thy faithfulness, Lord, unto me!" He understood something about God's love and mercies that are new every morning. And what is so amazing is that the old love and mercies are still ours. Great is his faithfulness!

Lord, keep me aware of and thankful for your great faithfulness. Amen.

Are You Hardheaded?

Ezekiel 3

But the house of Israel will not listen to you, for they are not willing to listen to me; because all the house of Israel have a hard forehead and a stubborn heart. (Ezekiel 3:7)

❧

I remember being called hardheaded as a child. That usually meant that I had done something that I specifically had been told not to do. One time I asked my mother to cut my hair so that I could have bangs. She told me that I did not need bangs and that I really should not cut my hair. Well, I did it anyway, and the results were disastrous. I somehow managed to get the comb tangled in my bangs, and the comb had to be cut out. I had a headache for days. My mother simply said, "Didn't I tell you not to do that?" As I grew older, I tried not to be so hardheaded. If my mother advised against something, I usually did not do it, fearing another disaster.

Like me, the people of Israel were hardheaded and stubborn. They had not learned their lesson. They had not listened to God, and God knew that they would not listen to Ezekiel. But Ezekiel was told to go anyway. He was to say to them, " 'Thus says the Lord GOD'; whether they hear or refuse to hear" (3:11*b*).

I would not have wanted Ezekiel's job. No one wants to go to speak to a rebellious and stubborn people, but God wants us to anyway. When our children, our spouses, and our bosses or employees will not listen, we are encouraged to speak God's message anyway. In order to speak God's message successfully, we must know that message. Sometimes people don't listen to us because they do not believe we know what we are talking about.

Are you secure enough in the word of God to speak to a hardheaded and stubborn people? Or are you too hardheaded and stubborn to respond to God's call to go?

Lord, remove the hardhead that I sometimes have, and make me obedient to your direction. Amen.

ARE YOUR BONES DRY?

EZEKIEL 37

Then he said to me, "Prophesy to these bones, and say to them: O dry bones, hear the word of the LORD." (Ezekiel 37:4)

In the black church, the worst thing one could experience was a dry or dead worship service. This meant that there was a silent, almost sleepy service. Everyone was quiet and unresponsive. The choirs and worship leaders seemed to be politely going through the motions of worship. The preacher read his manuscript, the offering was taken, no one responded to the invitation to Christian discipleship, and everyone went home. That was dry.

The service was alive when the congregation was responsive to everything that happened. They stood and waved their hands when the choir sang; they said "Amen" when the preacher read the scripture and preached the word (without a manuscript), and they shouted and cried as visitors came forward to unite with the church. That was alive.

Ezekiel had been lamenting over the sins of Israel. They had strayed so far from God that they seemed to exist in a valley of dry bones. There was no worship, no obedience to God's ordinances, and no reverence for his name. Ezekiel had exhausted his prophecies. He did not know how to proceed, so God set him down in the middle of a valley of dry bones. God asked him, "Can these bones live?" Ezekiel responded, "O Lord GOD, you know" (37:3).

Ezekiel had sense enough to know that if it was possible for dry bones to live, God could make it happen. Those dry bones took on flesh and came to life. They represented the whole house of Israel. God put his spirit in them, they responded to his word, and they were alive.

Are you dead or alive in your worship of God? Are your bones dry and unresponsive, or do they get up and move around. God desires alive worship!

Lord, breathe on me the breath of life so that I may worship you with a joyful and alive spirit! Amen.

No Matter What

Daniel 3

But if not, be it known to you, O king, that we will not serve your gods and we will not worship the golden statue that you have set up.
(Daniel 3:18)

❧

The three Hebrew boys, Shadrach, Meshach, and Abednego, refused to worship the golden statue that King Nebuchadnezzar had set up. They understood the consequences of their refusal. A fiery furnace awaited them, but they were determined not to bow down to that statue no matter what. They knew that the God they served was able to deliver them from what appeared to be a sure and painful death, but even if their God did not deliver them, they would not bow down. It did not matter to them whether God would save them because they knew that he was able to if he wanted. They knew they served a mighty God who could do whatever he wanted whenever he wanted, and they prayed that he did want to!

Why were these boys so brave and faithful? We know that they were disciplined, for rather than eating the royal rations, they ate only vegetables and drank only water. Even with their limited diet, they were stronger, healthier, and better looking than other young men in the palace. They were friends with Daniel who had insight into all visions and dreams, and God gave them knowledge and skill in every aspect of literature and wisdom (1:12-17). They were well grounded in their faith. A fiery furnace meant nothing to them because they knew that no image deserved their worship. They were committed to God alone.

What are the golden images to which we bow down? Often we bow down willingly—even without the threat of a fiery furnace. Name your images, those things that claim your devotion. Could they save you from a fiery furnace? I don't think so. But God can. Worship him no matter what!

Father, help me remove all of the golden images and statues in my life. You are the only one worthy of my devotion. Amen.

Shut by an Angel

Daniel 6

My God sent his angel and shut the lions' mouths so that they would not hurt me, because I was found blameless before him; and also before you, O king, I have done no wrong. (Daniel 6:22)

Darius the Mede became king after Belshazzar and had great respect for Daniel. In fact, he made Daniel one of his three presidents, and Daniel distinguished himself in such a way that the king wanted to appoint him over the whole kingdom. This pending appointment was not pleasing to other presidents and officials, so they plotted against Daniel. But Daniel was faithful to God and without corruption.

The presidents and officials knew that they had to come up with something that was related to

Daniel's worship of and devotion to his God, so they convinced the king to establish an ordinance forbidding worship of anyone but him. All violators of the ordinance would be thrown into a den of lions.

Although Daniel was fully aware of the ordinance, he boldly bowed down three times a day in view of all who cared to observe and worshiped and prayed to his God. Of course his actions were reported to the king, and he was thrown into a den of lions. But that same God to whom Daniel boldly prayed sent his angel to shut the mouths of the lions so that Daniel was not harmed.

Isn't it interesting that when we excel in our work and devotion, others plot against us? We must prepare for their treachery and hold fast to our faith. Daniel teaches us what it means to be bold witnesses for God. I wonder how many of us would have prayed in front of an open window, knowing that we had been forbidden to do so. Well, even though we have freedom of religion, we still are afraid to be bold for God. Let's change that!

Holy Father, keep us faithful to you against all odds and in spite of all circumstances. You still have angels who can shut the mouths of the lions who seek to harm us. Amen.

THE FAITHLESS LOVER

HOSEA 3

The LORD said to me again, "Go, love a woman who has a lover and is an adulteress, just as the LORD loves the people of Israel, though they turn to other gods and love raisin cakes." (Hosea 3:1)

God told Hosea—not just once, but twice—to take a wife who surely would be unfaithful. What an awesome directive! Many are afraid to take wives who they believe will not be faithful until they are parted by death, but Hosea is to take a wife who will start out unfaithful. God explained to Hosea that he must love this woman who had other lovers and children by other men, for in so doing, he would demonstrate God's love for a faithless people.

We like to think of love the way Elizabeth Barrett Browning did: "I love thee with the breath, / Smiles, tears of all my life! And, if God choose, / I shall but love thee better after death." But is that view of love realistic? Was that the kind of love that God instructed Hosea to give his wife realistic? He had to love her with the breath, smiles, and tears of all his life, and he probably loved her with tears a lot. I am sure that God loves us with tears more than with smiles, for we, like the people of Israel, often turn to other gods and love raisin cakes.

What is the significance of the raisin cakes? They were used as love offerings in pagan festal worship and represented the delicacies of the day. The people had placed their love on these external and material benefits of religion rather than on devotion to God. Again, they are like us. We may have choirs or robes or preachers who represent our raisin cakes. We spend our time worshiping them and not God. Even if we consider ourselves faithful in worship, our faithfulness disappears if our choir or our favorite preacher is not present. They truly represent our raisin cakes.

Hosea is challenged to take a wife and lead her to repentance so that she loves only him. It does not matter that she has been with other men; she is still worthy of redemption, and so are we.

Father, we thank you for your unconditional love. Make us worthy. Amen.

Poured-out Spirit

Joel 2

Then afterward I will pour out my spirit on all flesh; your sons and your daughters shall prophesy, your old men shall dream dreams, and your young men shall see visions. (Joel 2:28)

❧

Joel tells of the ruin of God's land and nation caused by the faithlessness of the people. The locusts have eaten the grain, and there is no wine, oil, or figs. Joel challenges the people to weep, repent, fast, and pray. He is so intent on relaying this message that he boldly announces, "Blow the trumpet in Zion; sound the alarm on my holy mountain! Let all the inhabitants of the land tremble, for the day of the Lord is coming, it is near" (2:1).

How would we respond if our food and drink

were suddenly cut off? Would there be a Joel around to blow the trumpet and sound the alarm, or would we use our resources to find food and drink elsewhere? Would we really believe that God had ruined the land because the people no longer served him? Who would listen to those prophets who tell us to return to the Lord with all our hearts and not our possessions? Who would proclaim, "Return to the LORD, your God, for he is gracious and merciful, slow to anger, and abounding in steadfast love, and relents from punishing" (2:13*b*)?

Once the trumpet was blown, the fast was sanctified, and the people were assembled, God had pity on them and sent them grain, wine, and oil. God let them know who was God and that there was no other. Then he poured out his spirit on them, and they were able to prophesy, dream dreams, and see visions. When God poured out his spirit, he did not skip women, for both sons and daughters would prophesy; and he did not skip the elderly, for old men would dream dreams. When God pours out his spirit, he is both generous and inclusive.

We must receive the spirit of God before we can prophesy, dream dreams, and see visions. Are we ready to receive the spirit?

Spirit of the living God, fall afresh on me. Amen.

Nothing but Justice and Righteousness

Amos 5

But let justice roll down like waters, and righteousness like an everflowing stream. (Amos 5:24)

❧

Amos was a shepherd from the hill country of Tekoa, about ten miles south of Jerusalem. The people to whom Amos prophesied were enjoying economic prosperity, and although they lived luxuriously, they were morally corrupt and worshiped idols. Amos, whose very name meant burden or burden-bearer, agreed to leave his simple life and accept the burden of warning the people of Israel of their sins.

Amos told the Israelites that God was not pleased with their festivals and assemblies. God did not accept their burnt offerings and grain offerings, and God was not listening to their music. All God wanted was for them to live in justice and righteousness.

Wouldn't it be wonderful to live in a world that flowed with justice and righteousness? We could forget about the rich hiring clever lawyers and getting away with numerous crimes, while the poor are punished in disproportionate numbers. We would not have to worry about affirmative-action laws to make universities and corporations accept minority students and employees. We could count on everyone to be fair and just and always do what is right. What a wonderful world that would be.

But we do not live in such a world, and neither justice nor righteousness flow freely. Is there an Amos willing to stand up for God and call us into repentance? Is there anyone who will tell us that we are morally corrupt and worship idols? Is there anyone brave enough to tell us that God does not like our festivals and music? Are you the one? If you are, start where you live. Let justice and righteousness roll down like water in your home, and let your home be a place of their everflowing stream.

Lord, help me lift Amos's burden and call my brothers and sisters to repentance. Amen.

Deeds Returned

Obadiah

For the day of the LORD is near against all the nations. As you have done, it shall be done to you; your deeds shall return on your own head.
(Obadiah 15)

❧

Obadiah, whose name means worshiper or servant of Yahweh, describes the sins of the Edomites in this short book. Edom failed to render aid to Israel during their wilderness experience and during their invasion by strangers. Edom stood silently and gloated over Israel's misfortune. Obadiah prophesies that the Lord will bring them down even though, for now, they soar aloft like eagles and their nest is set among the stars (v. 4).

The lesson here is very clear. We reap what we sow. What we do will be returned to us. That is the

Golden Rule, but it seems as though many do not believe in it. Maybe it is because we see so many people who seem to prosper from the con games they play on others. Maybe it is because we know people that get away with cheating and stealing. We want to know how long they will go unpunished. It is not for us to question when their deeds will be returned on their heads. We must be aware that someday, in God's own time, those deeds will be returned.

So, what are we to do? Obadiah charges us not to slaughter and kill. He tells us to come forward when we see others stealing. He reminds us not to gloat over the misfortunes of others. He challenges us not to loot and steal when others are being plundered and that we should not help the enemy by turning over those who manage to survive the enemy's invasion.

These directives apply to us today as we hear about looting, rioting, and stealing after earthquakes, fires, and other tragedies. These also apply to those who survive school shootings and terrorist attacks. Yes, Obadiah clearly is talking to us. Our deeds shall be returned. The kingdom shall be the Lord's.

Father, keep us from the sins of the Edomites. Amen.

RIGHTEOUS ANGER

JONAH 4

And the LORD said, "Is it right for you to be angry?" (Jonah 4:4)

❧

Jonah did not want to carry out the assignment given to him. He knew how sinful the people of Nineveh were, but he also knew that God was merciful and probably would forgive them. I guess Jonah thought he would be wasting his time preaching to them if God would forgive them anyway.

So Jonah went the other way. He disobeyed God, but God knew how to get his attention. Jonah was cast into the sea and then given time to reflect while in the belly of a fish. Realizing that God meant for him to go to Nineveh regardless of his feelings, Jonah finally obeyed.

Jonah told the Ninevites that in forty days they would be overthrown. The Ninevites listened. They fasted, put on sackcloth, and repented of their evil ways. God considered their repentance and did not bring calamity on them.

Jonah did not like this one bit. He cried to God that he knew all along that the Ninevites would be forgiven, and that was the very reason he did not want to go to them in the first place. Jonah was so angry that he asked to die.

God demonstrated his concern for Nineveh by causing a bush to grow and provide shade for Jonah. Jonah was grateful for the bush. But God caused the bush to be removed, and Jonah was angry. Yet, God made Jonah realize that being angry about the destruction of a bush Jonah neither labored for nor grew and which came and then disappeared in a night could not compare with God's feelings about the great city of Nineveh. Jonah had no reason to be angry. God chose to save those he loved over the years.

Is our anger ever righteous and justified? Think about it. Why do we get angry about things we have no control over? God is in charge. Trust him!

Lord, remove the angry feelings that sometimes cloud my vision and worship of you. Amen.

War No More

Micah 4

He shall judge between many peoples, and shall arbitrate between strong nations far away; they shall beat their swords into plowshares, and their spears into pruning hooks; nation shall not lift up sword against nation, neither shall they learn war any more. (Micah 4:3)

Micah is given the awesome task of pronouncing judgment on the people of Jerusalem. The rich have abused the poor and used their positions of power for personal gain. Micah tells them that the Lord God will be a witness against them (1:2*b*), and because their rulers give judgments for a bribe and their teachers and prophets are only interested in being paid, Jerusalem will become a heap of ruins (3:11-12).

Micah prophesies of a future day when the Lord's house will be raised high, and all people will go there to worship and walk in God's ordinances. When that occurs, there will be no more war. There will be neither violence nor need for swords or spears. Those former weapons of violence will become instruments used to rebuild God's nation.

Wouldn't it be wonderful if we as a nation would stop abusing the poor and using powerful positions for personal gain? What if our rulers never accepted bribes and our teachers and leaders never worried about how much they were paid? If that happened, we would be in a position to lift the house and worship of the Lord high.

The day of no more war can come only when we lift the worship of the Lord God high. It is in love and peace that we lift God high. It is in fairness and concern that we obey God's ordinances. It is in turning in our guns and weapons of war that we cease to live in fear.

What can you do today to put down your weapons of war and live in peace?

Lord, I want to be one of your faithful servants who lives in that place where there is no more war. Amen.

EVIL REPAID

NAHUM 3

There is no assuaging your hurt, your wound is mortal. All who hear the news about you clap their hands over you. For who has ever escaped your endless cruelty? (Nahum 3:19)

❦

It is interesting to note that the name Nahum means comfort. Who is being comforted by Nahum's message? It certainly cannot be the people of Nineveh, for even after they had repented upon hearing Jonah's reluctant message, they had returned to their evil ways. How could Nineveh forget the sackcloth and ashes they had worn to express their remorse? Somehow they did. They returned to violence, idolatry, and arrogance. I suppose they thought that God would keep forgiving them. They somehow mistook his mercy for foolishness.

❦

But Nahum knew that God is not foolish, and he did not offer comfort. He preached that God is jealous, avenging, and wrathful. God rages against his enemies and will not clear the guilty (1:2). God promises to destroy and bury the idols the people have been worshiping because they are worthless (1:14). He lets them know that they are mortally wounded and that all who hear of their calamity are rejoicing.

But there is comfort for Judah; God will restore Israel. Judah is told to celebrate their festivals and fulfill their vows. The wicked will never again invade them; their enemies are cut off (1:15). The Gentile people of Nineveh had their chance to be faithful to God, but they blew it.

Could Nahum be preaching to us? How often have we blown the chances that God has given us? Have we repented and then returned to our sinful ways? Are others looking at us and rejoicing over our difficulties? Can't you just hear them saying, "See what happens to so-called Christians? Their God has deserted them because they have done such cruel acts."

Father, please send Nahum to comfort us. We, like the people of Nineveh, deserve punishment for our evil deeds, but we want to be like Judah, restored and celebrating and fulfilling our vows. Amen.

Write the Vision

Habakkuk 2

For there is still a vision for the appointed time; it speaks of the end, and does not lie. If it seems to tarry, wait for it; it will surely come, it will not delay. (Habakkuk 2:3)

Judah again has fallen by the wayside, and Habakkuk complains to God about the injustices that surround him. This nation just does not get it. They are cruel and wicked, evil and destructive, unfair and violent, and Habakkuk is tired of preaching for change.

Habakkuk's complaints could be those of any Christian serious about seeing its nation live up to its Christian foundation. Today's preachers and prophets could raise the same questions with God: "O LORD, how long shall I cry for help, and you will not listen?" (1:2). I know that many modern-day Christians wonder why God is not doing something about the evil and violence that abound.

God answers Habakkuk by telling him to write the vision and to make it so plain that a runner passing by could read it. Habakkuk is God's prophet, and he knows the vision. God has revealed it to him. It is Habakkuk's duty to write that vision down and communicate it to the nation. No matter how evil the nation has become, there is still a vision of truth for the appointed time. Even if it seems to be long in coming, it will surely come (2:3).

Is God telling us the same thing? Look around at the sins of the world, and you write the vision. You tell your brothers and sisters what God wants them to do. You make it plain so that anyone running by can read it. You let them know that God's truth will be, that he will reclaim his people. Even if it seems a long time in coming, it will come.

Are you equipped to write the vision? Habakkuk was, and he did. Will you?

Lord, reveal your vision to me, and I promise that I will write and uphold it. Amen.

Silver and Gold Can't Save Us

Zephaniah 1

Neither their silver nor their gold will be able to save them on the day of the Lord's wrath; in the fire of his passion the whole earth shall be consumed; for a full, a terrible end he will make of all the inhabitants of the earth. (Zephaniah 1:18)

During the reign of King Josiah, many reforms were instituted. Josiah was a good king who was greatly distressed that Judah had strayed so far from the worship of God.

King Josiah sought to verify a book of law found in the temple. He needed to know whether that book was indeed the authentic word of God. He called on the prophetess Huldah who authenticated the book. (This book was later recognized as the book of Deuteronomy.) Huldah spoke for God, and she told Josiah that what was contained in the book was the word of God.

It was obvious that Judah had begun to worship idols, and Zephaniah preached that a change of heart was needed. Judah began to make some outward changes because of the reforms that Josiah instituted, but Zephaniah was convinced that the hearts of the people still were corrupt. He could see that Judah had placed its faith in silver and gold. Zephaniah told the people in no uncertain terms that neither silver nor gold would save them.

I wonder whether we have placed our faith in silver and gold. Sometimes we believe that if we have enough money, we can buy our way out of trouble or improve our status or reputation. We may even believe that if we have enough money, we can convince that prestigious school to admit our wayward children.

We, like Judah, need the type of reform that comes from a change of heart. Neither silver nor gold will save us.

Lord, give me a pure heart free from the corruption that surrounds me daily so that I may serve you. Amen.

THE TIME IS NOW!

HAGGAI 1

Thus says the LORD of hosts: These people say the time has not yet come to rebuild the LORD's house. (Haggai 1:2)

❧

The people of Judah had returned from their Babylonian exile. They should have been busy worshiping and praising God, but they were consumed with their own affairs. They had been given the task of rebuilding God's temple in Jerusalem, but they instead built their own houses while God's house remained in ruins. Although the work of rebuilding the temple had begun, after sixteen years, it was still unfinished. Haggai was sent to preach to them and to let them know that God was not pleased.

Haggai reminded Judah of the futility of their

efforts. They had sown much, but harvested little. They spent their time eating and drinking, but never were full. Their clothes never warmed them, and their wages did not increase their wealth. Haggai told them to consider how they had fared. Didn't they get it? God was not blessing them.

The people cried that the time had not yet come to rebuild the temple, but Haggai reminded them that they had taken the time to build their own houses. If it was the time for them, then it certainly was the time for God.

How many of us put off God's work? We say that when our children are older or when we retire or when we have more money we will give more time to God. Well, tomorrow never comes. We have to heed Haggai's warning and consider how we have fared? Is the work that we are doing prospering? Is God blessing our efforts, or are we just spinning our wheels?

I once was told by a student who was accustomed to putting off assignments until the very last minute that she had elevated procrastination to an art form. Well, procrastination does not deserve to be an art form! It needs to be eliminated. Now is the time for God's work and for our own. Start now to rebuild God's and your own temples!

Lord, help me act out my commitment to you right now. Amen.

Turning a Deaf Ear

Zechariah 7

They made their hearts adamant in order not to hear the law and the words that the Lord of hosts had sent by his spirit through the former prophets. Therefore great wrath came from the Lord of hosts. (Zechariah 7:12)

❧

Have you ever felt that someone was turning a deaf ear to your advice and counsel? I certainly have. I have often warned my younger son about the people he associates with, his failing to be faithful in church attendance and worship, and his developing good study habits and work ethics. But he seems to turn a deaf ear. I find myself repeating the same lecture or, as he calls it, the same sermon over and over again. How like the people of Judah he is.

God must have been tired of pleading with Judah to obey his laws. God sent prophet after prophet to deliver his message. Haggai had told them that they had to spend the time necessary to rebuild God's temple, but they kept putting it off. They saw that they were not progressing in their personal lives, yet they still refused to do God's work. Then Zechariah tried a new approach. He reminded them to be fair in their judgments, to be kind and merciful to one another, to refrain from oppressing the widows, orphans, aliens, and the poor, and to refrain from devising evil against one another (7:9-10). But even with these explicit instructions, Judah turned a deaf ear. "But they refused to listen, and turned a stubborn shoulder, and stopped their ears in order not to hear" (7:11).

To what great heights we go to be disobedient. We want to claim ignorance when we simply refuse to listen. What message delivered by one of God's servants do you refuse to hear? Is there a sick or elderly person you are told to visit? Is there a ministry at church that needs your expertise? How are you putting off building the temple?

God has warned us. He is a jealous God, and if we continue to turn away from him, disaster awaits. Listen; God is speaking to you!

Father, open my ears that I may hear what you are saying. Amen.

No Respect

Malachi 1 and 2

*A son honors his father, and servants their master.
If then I am a father, where is the honor due me?
And if I am a master, where is the respect due
me? says the LORD of hosts to you, O priests, who
despise my name. You say, "How have we
despised your name?" (Malachi 1:6)*

Malachi, whose name means my messenger, is the last of the Old Testament prophets. God is so displeased with his chosen people that he does not send them another messenger for four hundred years, and that messenger is John the Baptist who prepares the way for Jesus the Christ.

Malachi tries a new approach in communicating with the Israelites. He uses questions. He tells them that God asks where his honor and respect are and why his name is despised. Of course the corrupt priests who answer for the people act like they do not know what Malachi is talking about. In other words, they play dumb, and Malachi has to spell it out.

Malachi has a straightforward message for them; he tells them that they have polluted the Lord's Table with imperfect sacrifices; they have been faithless and profaned the sanctuary; and they have married the daughters of foreign gods. God is ready to put them out of his presence. Even though Malachi is very clear, they still ask where the God of justice is.

How like the Israelites we often are. We, too, give God imperfect offerings. We give what we don't want. We offer the last of our abundance, the leftover portion of our time, and the briefest moments of praise and thanksgiving. Then, when things don't go our way, we ask, "Where is the God of justice?"

God deserves our respect. He is our father, our master, the controller of our lives. Why do we despise his name by not offering him our best? The new messenger who Malachi predicted has already come. Don't we hear him?

Lord, I don't want to be put from your presence. Teach me to show the respect you deserve. Amen.

WHAT GIFT DO YOU BRING?

MATTHEW 2:1-12

On entering the house, they saw the child with Mary his mother; and they knelt down and paid him homage. Then, opening their treasure chests, they offered him gifts of gold, frankincense, and myrrh. (Matthew 2:11)

Unlike Herod, who feared that this newborn king would interfere with his own position of power and influence, the wise men searched for the child and, in worship and reverence, offered gifts. Let us look closely at those gifts.

There is gold, a gift fit for a king. What is finer than pure gold? It never tarnishes but retains its luster. This newborn king, reigning from a cross, not a throne, will not tarnish through the many years to come; he also will retain his luster. He is the king of kings. He is worthy of pure gold.

Then there is frankincense, a gift for a priest. Priests used frankincense in temple worship and sacrifices. This priest of all priests will show us what true worship is, and he will become the ultimate sacrifice. What a fitting gift! Last is myrrh, a gift for one who is to die. Myrrh was used to embalm the bodies of the dead, and it was known from Jesus' birth that he would give his life for the sins of the world. A real king would die to save his subjects. The wise men knew he would be a real king.

What gift can we bring to the Christ? We can offer our gold or monies to build houses of worship, to sponsor programs of Christian service, and to help those who are in need. If we truly are offering our gold, why are there so many homeless people around us? Well, perhaps we are offering frankincense, our worship and sacrifice. If we are, why are so many churches empty, and why are we so selfish? Surely we are offering our myrrh, our willingness to die for each other. If we are, why are more lives taken than saved?

Think about the gift you can bring. If you give your heart, all of the other gifts you might offer will be included.

Lord, I offer my heart to Jesus, my Savior and King. Amen.

ARE YOU A FISHER OF MEN AND WOMEN?

MATTHEW 4:18-22

And he said to them, "Follow me, and I will make you fish for people." (Matthew 4:19)

❧

What does it take to be a good fisherman? I know that a fisherman must be patient. I remember going fishing when I was a child, and the hardest thing was to wait for the fish to bite. Sometimes I would wait all day and catch nothing. Yet, even after what seemed to be a wasted day, I would go back and try again another day. In addition to being patient, the good fisherman must be willing to try and try again. When you are trying to fish for men and women and introduce them to Christ, are you patient and persevering?

❧

You must have courage to be a good fisherman. A good fisherman is a good swimmer, for he knows there is danger in the water. He or she must be able to swim even if the water is rough and deep. What about us? Do we go only after men and women who are easy to catch? Easy catches are those who recently have moved to town and have not yet joined a church but were active where they used to live. But are we willing to fish for those who do not believe in organized religion and have no use for it? It will take courage to fish for these unsaved persons.

We also must be at the right place at the right time and use the right bait. A good fisherman knows the best time and place to cast his net, and knows what bait to use. Do we? Do we know the right time and place to invite others to worship with us? Do we sense their hours of need and offer them Jesus, or do we visit when they are not interested in what we have to offer? Our timing and our bait must be right if we are to be good fishers of men and women.

The first men Jesus called were already working. They knew how to fish, so they did not need to be trained. If we are already trying to lead others to Christ, we know what it takes to be successful. We need to encourage others to become fishers of men and women.

Lord, I want to be a good fisherman for you. Amen.

Plain Vanilla

Matthew 5:1-11

Blessed are the pure in heart, for they will see God. (Matthew 5:8)

This beatitude always reminds me of children. I think of children as being pure in heart, for they are young, innocent, uncorrupted, or what I call plain vanilla. They have not lived long enough to start adding all the fruits, nuts, and syrups, to create the various flavors that bring contamination to their lives. They are pure, plain vanilla, and they can see God.

I remember the story of a little girl who welcomed a new baby sister into the family. She kept hanging around the nursery, waiting for a moment to be alone with the new baby. The mother was concerned about this hovering and was just about to ask her older daughter to move away from the crib when she heard the girl ask the baby, "What is God like? I have been away from him so long that I have forgotten." The little girl knew that the pure in heart do see God.

How can we be pure in heart? Our motives must be pure. That means we always must seek to lift up God in everything we do; we can have no hidden agendas or secret purposes in our dealings with one another. We must give generously from our hearts with no thought of receiving credit or praise or of having our names listed on some gold roster. When we give from our hearts, we need neither thanks nor acknowledgment.

Being pure in heart also means serving God because God is worthy to be served. How often do politicians and others attend church and serve so that they can win votes or get good jobs? Are our motives pure, or are we networking? How many of those serving God represent contaminated flavors?

Let us strive today to remove all of the additives that keep us from being pure. We must be pure vanilla, washed in the blood of the Lamb, if we are to see God.

Father, help me become like a little child so that I may enter the Kingdom of heaven. Amen.

JUST SAY THE WORD

MATTHEW 8:5-13

The centurion answered, "Lord, I am not worthy to have you come under my roof; but only speak the word, and my servant will be healed."
(Matthew 8:8)

❧

Great crowds followed Jesus after he had preached the Sermon on the Mount. It seemed that he had made a good impression, and many wanted to be healed of their various illnesses. It did not matter that he had told those cured not to tell anyone about him. His fame followed him, and more and more people sought his help.

There was a centurion, a leader of men, who had great authority. He was accustomed to giving orders and having them obeyed. Whatever he commanded was complied with. So, when he sought Jesus to cure his servant, he knew that all Jesus had to do was say the word. Yet, Jesus took the time to respond to the centurion. He told him that he would go to the centurion's house and touch his servant so that he would no longer be paralyzed and distressed. This response was unexpected. The centurion knew that Jesus was a great man, and he felt unworthy to have Jesus enter his home. He explained that even someone like himself could say words and have them obeyed, so he knew that a person as powerful as Jesus could certainly say the word and affect a cure.

Jesus had not found such faith in all of Israel. It was a special kind of witness. First, the centurion was not asking for himself or for a family member; he was asking for a servant, a person of low standing in the community. Second, the centurion did not feel worthy to have Jesus under his roof; although he was a man of authority, he was not equal to Jesus. He was not even a Jew. Third, the centurion knew that Jesus' words were powerful; if he had the power to say words and have them obeyed, then Jesus had the power to say words and have healing take place.

Do we have the kind of special faith and witness that is unselfish, humble, and powerful?

Lord, I want the faith of the centurion. Amen.

DO YOU WANT TO BE COUNTED?

MATTHEW 14:13-21

And those who ate were about five thousand men, besides women and children. (Matthew 14:21)

❦

It is amazing to me that during biblical times, women often were not named or counted. If Jesus fed five thousand men, then he must have fed ten thousand women and children. We all know that most of the time there are twice as many women and children in church than there are men. Why didn't they count the women and children?

I remember hearing my mother talk about the people in our neighborhood. She told me that some of the people were forward-thinking and progressive while others were backward and up to no good. She described some who would make something out of their lives and others who probably would never amount to much. It was this latter type that she would label as "no count." When a person was "no count," I was to stay away because he or she surely would get me into trouble. No one wanted to be labeled as "no count."

Yet, the women and children were "no count." They were not important enough to be counted. Did this mean that they would never amount to much or that they were a source of trouble? I don't think so. I believe that the women and children were not valued. It was the men who were important, who were responsible for the welfare of the family, and who should be fed first. Even though this may have been the thinking of the day, we must remember that it was a child who had the five loaves and two fish. It was a little boy's lunch that his mother prepared. Without the boy and his mother, no one would have been fed.

I know that you and I want to be counted. We, like that little boy and his mother, are capable of being instruments for miracles. Who is it that we are failing to count or labeling as "no count"?

Father, count me as one of your children. I am eager to be used by you. Amen.

JUST THE CRUMBS

MATTHEW 15:21-28

She said, "Yes, Lord, yet even the dogs eat the crumbs that fall from their masters' table."
(Matthew 15:27)

❧

It is hard for me to imagine being bold enough or alert enough to have a powerful comeback to Jesus' statement, "It is not fair to take the children's food and throw it to the dogs" (15:26). Yet, the Canaanite woman did have such a powerful and faithful comeback.

This mother was in search of a cure for her demon-possessed daughter. This mother did not know Jesus, and she did not know his disciples. In fact, she did not live where they lived, and she was not of the same race and culture. She was a Canaanite, and they were Jews. She lived in the district of Tyre and Sidon, Gentile territory, and they lived in Jewish territory, around Jerusalem. She did not share their religion, but she had heard about Jesus. She was not concerned about whether she was worthy of this teacher's blessing; all she was concerned about was her daughter's healing.

So this desperate mother approached Jesus with humility. Although he was not her Lord, she called him Lord, Son of David. She must have known how important Jesus' ancestry was to the Jews, so she made sure she included it in her address. She begged for mercy and ignored the disciples' trying to send her away. She would not be denied. She was not asking for all that Jesus had come to provide for the lost sheep of Israel; all she needed were the crumbs of his healing power. She understood that crumbs would be enough. Even the dogs under the children's table were worthy of crumbs. She and her daughter were at least as good as the dogs, and Jesus was moved by her great faith. He healed her daughter instantly.

How great is our faith? Would we have been willing to accept the crumbs that are usually left for dogs? I wonder. But I am encouraged to know that although we may think we need a whole meal, crumbs are enough.

Lord, give me just the crumbs of that Canaanite woman's faith. With just that much, I can move mountains. Amen.

WHAT MUST I DO?

MATTHEW 19:16-30

Then someone came to him and said, "Teacher, what good deed must I do to have eternal life?"
(Matthew 19:16)

❧

Whenever I hear the question, "Teacher, what must I do?" I think of the college students I taught for ten years. Every semester I issued a course syllabus on the first day of class. The syllabus covered the subject matter for each class, the homework assignments, the days the tests would be given, and days the term papers would be due. Each student knew what he or she had to do; yet, near the end of the semester, they would come to me and ask the same question.

I always felt like Jesus speaking to the rich young ruler. I would tell them that they had known from the first day what the requirements were. And if they had fulfilled them, then they would pass the class. I would tell them that I could not save them if they had not done their work. Often, like the rich young ruler, they would go away sorrowful.

The rich young ruler was told that he had to keep the commandments, and he asked, "Which ones?" It appears that he did not believe that he had to keep all of them. Some of them must have been more important than others. My students also wanted to know if they had to complete all of the assignments and take all of the tests. Somehow they believed that some of these assignments were just busy work and did not need to be completed.

Jesus answered the young man's question by naming the commandments that had to do with relationships—adultery, stealing, lying, honoring, and loving. These particular commandments were emphasized because it is impossible to show love for God if we do not love our fellow man. Although the young ruler felt confident that he had kept these commandments from his youth, he was not willing to give up his possessions. Like my students, he was challenged to complete all of the assignments and take all of the tests. What must you do?

Lord, you've shown me the requirements; help me pass the test. Amen.

Be Prepared!

Matthew 25:1-13

And while they went to buy it, the bridegroom came, and those who were ready went with him into the wedding banquet; and the door was shut.
(Matthew 25:10)

❧

How often are we caught unprepared? Our lack of preparation may appear in our cooking a meal and discovering that we are out of a much-needed ingredient. Our lack of preparation may appear in our desiring to wear a particular outfit and discovering that it needs to be cleaned. Our lack of preparation may even hit us as we read the test questions and realize that we have not studied the right material. There are so many ways that we can be caught unprepared.

The foolish virgins were unprepared. They had not

bothered to take oil with them, and the bridegroom was delayed and did not arrive until midnight. By that time, everyone was asleep, but the wise virgins were able to awaken, trim their lamps with the oil they had brought with them, and go out to meet the bridegroom. The foolish virgins were unprepared. They even asked the wise virgins to share their oil with them, but the wise virgins realized that if they shared their oil, there would not be enough for all of them. They suggested that the foolish virgins buy their own oil. Of course, while these foolish virgins were gone, the bridegroom took those who were prepared with him, and the wedding banquet door was shut. Once the door was shut, no one could enter.

This parable speaks to us today. We never know what is going to happen next, and we need to be prepared as best we can. If it means stocking the pantry with the ingredients we need to prepare our meals or cleaning our clothes so that they are ready when we need them or studying sufficiently to pass tests, we must be prepared. Yet, the most essential preparation of all is to be ready to meet the Master. How are we preparing for that? The forerunner has already come. He has told us what is required. Are we listening? Are we prepared? Be ready, for you know neither the day nor the hour.

Lord, I want to be ready to walk in Jerusalem, just like John. Amen.

HAVE YOU EVER WASHED YOUR HANDS?

MATTHEW 27:11-26

So when Pilate saw that he could do nothing, but rather that a riot was beginning, he took some water and washed his hands before the crowd, saying, "I am innocent of this man's blood; see to it yourselves." (Matthew 27:24)

❧

Pilate did everything he could not to be involved in the crucifixion of Jesus. When Jesus was first brought before him, Pilate asked if Jesus was the King of the Jews. This question was necessary because claiming to be a king was a political charge, and the only official charge against Jesus was blasphemy, which was a religious charge. If that was the only charge, then Pilate could say that he had no jurisdiction over religious charges. But Jesus' accusers made sure that there were political charges so that Pilate would have to deal with Jesus. Jesus was charged with claiming to be a king, being a revolutionary, and inciting the people not to pay taxes. Pilate had to deal with those charges.

Pilate's wife warned him not to have anything to do with this innocent man. She had had a dream about him and did not want her husband involved in this crucifixion. She was bold enough to send him a note while he was sitting on the judgment seat. She did not want him to take her warning lightly. But Pilate could not tell the people that he would not deal with Jesus because his wife told him not to.

Pilate tried one last thing. He knew that it was customary during the Passover festival to release any prisoner the crowd selected. He asked if they wanted him to release Jesus, the Messiah, or Barabbas, a known criminal. He had hoped that they would choose Jesus, but they did not. They demanded that Jesus be killed. So Pilate washed his hands of the matter.

How often have we washed our hands of some matter that we could not control? Do we simply give up and let an unruly and misinformed crowd have its way? Do we dare take a stand and keep fighting for what we know is right? Think about it before you wash your hands!

Lord, give me the courage to get my hands dirty. Washing them is the coward's way out. Amen.

Are You a Forerunner?

Mark 1:1-11

As it is written in the prophet Isaiah, "See, I am sending my messenger ahead of you, who will prepare your way; the voice of one crying out in the wilderness; 'Prepare the way of the Lord, make his paths straight.' " (Mark 1:2)

❧

How often have you wished that someone had prepared the way for you? Wouldn't it have been nice to have a model or example of what was expected and what could be accomplished? Yet, so often we are called on to be the forerunner, the one who prepares the way, the mentor.

Many times I have had to be the forerunner. I often was the first African American hired in a professional position during my years in Corporate America. I mentored other African Americans who were hired and had questions about the possibilities for advancement. I always tried to encourage these young professionals, but after twenty-eight years, I decided the corporate world was just not for me. But I like to think that I was a forerunner. I hope that it was easier for my former companies to hire minorities and to have confidence that their work would exceed all expectations.

John was a forerunner. Although he prepared the way by introducing the Lord, he could not make the job that awaited Jesus any easier. John introduced baptism by water, but Jesus brought baptism by the Holy Spirit. John had disciples who accompanied him as he went about, but Jesus taught his disciples to teach, preach, heal, and courageously die for their faith. John prepared the way, but Jesus was the Way!

We, too, can be forerunners. We can prepare the way for those who follow us, but we cannot do their work for them or even make that work easier. All we can do is leave a model they can build upon and help create a receptive atmosphere so that they are not working in a hostile environment. Are you willing to be a forerunner? John was.

Lord, I want to help prepare the hearts of men and women to receive Jesus. Make me a forerunner. Amen.

The Power of Talking to Yourself

Mark 5:21-34

For she said, "If I but touch his clothes, I will be made well." (Mark 5:28)

❧

Have you ever had a heart-to-heart conversation with yourself? You may have had to convince yourself to do something that you knew you had the ability to do or to avoid some action. Sometimes you may have had to argue with yourself a little. One side of you wanted to do one thing while the other side knew that it was not in your best interest.

The woman in today's scripture did some talking to herself. She had been ill for twelve years, and although she had been to many doctors and had spent all of her resources, she had not gotten any better. In fact, she had gotten worse. She heard about Jesus and decided that he was the doctor that she needed. Her problem was that she could not get to him. He was passing nearby, but the crowds were so pressed around him that she could not get close enough to ask for his healing power. She talked to and convinced herself that all she had to do was touch something that was touching him. She did not even have to touch him; his clothes would do.

So she pressed through the crowd even while Jesus was being rushed away to heal the daughter of a synagogue leader. Finally, she was close enough to touch his clothes, and immediately she was healed.

Jesus felt the healing power leave his body, and he knew that someone had touched him. When the woman identified herself, he told her to go in peace, for her faith had made her well.

What act of faith do you need to talk to yourself about today? Are you bold enough to move forward through the crowded issues of life? Are you faithful enough to know that Jesus is always with you and that you can touch him anytime and anywhere? Talk yourself into reaching out to touch him, and be healed.

Lord, I need the power of your healing touch today. Amen.

WHAT GOD HAS JOINED

MARK 10:1-12

Therefore what God has joined together, let no one separate. (Mark 10:9)

❧

Many times I have attended weddings and heard my husband as pastor say, "What God has joined together let neither man nor woman put asunder. And if you agree with that say, 'Amen.'" The wedding guests always respond with a humorous "Amen," but I wonder if they are really thinking about what they are responding to. The "Amen" literally means let it be so; it affirms the statement that has been made. We as wedding guests are saying that we will not separate the couple and will not encourage anyone else to separate them. We believe that God has joined them and that they should stay that way until they are parted by death.

I meet so many young people today who enter into marriage with a plan B, the backup plan if the marriage does not work. Some couples sign prenuptial agreements so that neither mate can claim the previously owned possessions of the other. They may also have a backup house to move into, a backup job, or even a backup significant other. They have everything planned for failure.

Perhaps the couples that plan for failure have not been joined by God. If God has truly joined each to the other, they will make the marriage work. They will sacrifice when necessary; they will compromise; they will love unconditionally. They will do whatever it takes to keep the marriage together.

Whenever I have an opportunity to counsel couples that are engaged, I always talk to the bride and tell her to forget the 50-50 propositions. I want her to be prepared to give 90 percent and expect only 10 percent from her groom. If he should respond in the same way, they will have 180 percent invested in making their marriage work. Nothing would be able to separate two so heavily invested in their union.

Lord, bless marriages everywhere, and keep us aware that when we say "Amen" to what you have joined, we are praying for an eternal union. Amen.

The First Shout

Luke 1

When Elizabeth heard Mary's greeting, the child leaped in her womb. And Elizabeth was filled with the Holy Spirit. (Luke 1:41)

❧

Mary knew that her relative Elizabeth was pregnant and decided to share her own pregnancy with Elizabeth. Perhaps Mary wanted some advice, or perhaps she just wanted to share the joy of knowing that she was to be the mother of God's child. We do not know her real reason for visiting Elizabeth, but we know that she "went with haste" (1:39).

Mary must have entered Elizabeth's house saying something like, "Hello, is anyone home? It's Mary." Now Elizabeth was in her sixth month of pregnancy, and I know that women can feel the baby's movements at about four months. So Elizabeth was well aware of the child in her womb. When that child heard the greeting and sensed that he was in the presence of the Lord, he leaped in her womb. That, for me, was the first Holy Shout or loss of physical control from being overwhelmed by the Spirit of the Lord.

Elizabeth admitted that her child leaped for joy at the sound of her greeting. That child was the forerunner, and his mission was clear. The one for whom he was to prepare the path had arrived on the scene in the womb of his mother. The yet to be born, John, knew it, and so did Elizabeth. Elizabeth blessed her relative and acknowledged that what the Lord had spoken would be fulfilled through this birth. In fact, the speeches of both Elizabeth and Mary that are found in Luke are among the longest speeches by women in the Bible.

Have you ever felt the presence of the Lord so profoundly that you just could not sit still? I know I have. Sometimes I just have to stand up and wave my hand or wipe away the tears of joy, realizing that the Lord has granted me salvation.

John knew that salvation had come. He could not keep still even in the womb. Why is it that we keep our seats in the sanctuary?

Lord, fill me with your Holy Spirit, and don't restrain my leap for joy. Amen.

Making a Way

Luke 5:17-26

But finding no way to bring him in because of the crowd, they went up on the roof and let him down with his bed through the tiles into the middle of the crowd in front of Jesus. (Luke 5:19)

❧

If there ever was a case of finding a way or making one, I believe the situation in this scripture fits the bill. You see, everyone was crowding around Jesus. The scripture says that "the power of the Lord was with him to heal" (5:17b), and the crowd must have known it because they all wanted to be healed. One paralyzed man had some very faithful friends, for when they discovered that there was no way to bring him through the crowd to see Jesus, they took him to the roof and lowered him down in front of Jesus. They could not find a way, so they made one.

Jesus was so impressed with their faith that he told the paralytic that his sins were forgiven. This really shook everybody up. Why didn't Jesus just touch the man and heal his paralysis? Perhaps Jesus was using this instance to reveal that if we are sick in mind, we are also sick in body. We can be sick in mind through the weight of the guilt of sins that we carry around with us. Perhaps this is what Jesus saw in this man, and he knew that removing the guilt would heal his mind and consequently heal his body. But the scribes and Pharisees thought he was speaking blasphemy, for no one but God could forgive sins. Jesus let them know that he had the authority to forgive sins and that he could just as easily tell the man to stand and walk as he could tell him he was forgiven and healed in mind and body.

There seems to be an emphasis on the state of one's mind in this scripture. One must have a mind to find a way or make a way, and one must be freed in mind of the weight and guilt of sin. Sometimes finding a way to get to Jesus may be more than physical. We may not only have to push our way through a crowd, but we may also have to push our way through our sins. We can be assured that once we make our way to Jesus, he will forgive and heal us.

Lord, free my mind, remove my guilt, and heal me in body and spirit. Amen.

WHERE ARE THE OTHER NINE?

LUKE 17:11-19

Then Jesus asked, "Were not ten made clean? But the other nine, where are they?" (Luke 17:17)

❧

Have you ever failed to express your gratitude for a kindness shown to you? Sometimes we take kindness for granted or become involved in our daily activities and just forget to say "thank you." Those two words are so simple, and yet they express so much.

Ten lepers approached Jesus on his way to Jerusalem. They cried out to him and begged for mercy. They wanted to be made clean. Jesus did not hesitate in responding to them. He told them to go and show themselves to the priests, and while they were on their way, they were made clean.

We might think that the story of this cleansing ends here. The lepers cried for mercy, and Jesus healed them. But Jesus did not simply cleanse them; he gave them specific instructions. They were to go to the priests. They had to get involved in something just the way we become involved in our agendas. Jesus knew that once they were on their way and walked some distance from where he was, it would take some effort for them to return and give thanks. Perhaps it was just a test. How many of the ten would actually return?

We know that only one returned, and Jesus asked where the other nine were. I wonder whether we are included in that nine. Do we remember to give thanks daily for our many blessings, or are we so busy attending to our busy schedules that we forget? Just how busy are we really? What is it that takes up so much of our time? Like the lepers, we may be on our way somewhere that we feel the Lord has told us to go. We may be doing acts of kindness or working hard on a job God gave us. Even if we are doing something that God has told us to do, we still must take the time to return to him and offer praise and thanksgiving.

Lord, what is it that I have forgotten to thank you for today? I don't want to be one of the other nine! Amen.

The Squeaking Wheel

Luke 18:1-8

Yet because this widow keeps bothering me, I will grant her justice, so that she may not wear me out by continually coming. (Luke 18:5)

How many times have you felt like the judge in this story? You just get sick of someone bothering you, so you finally give in and give that person whatever is wanted. You just want that person to leave you alone. Or maybe you have bugged a company about a bad repair job, and just kept calling the company until they sent someone to do the job correctly. Your actions have proved that the squeaking wheel gets the oil.

The persistent widow in this parable was a squeaking wheel. Because her husband was dead, no one appealed for her against her opponents. She probably had been swindled out of means of support and was determined to get justice. Jesus uses her story to demonstrate that even an unjust judge who has no regard for God will eventually give in and grant a request if one is persistent. If an unjust judge would grant a request because he had been repeatedly asked to, would not a just God answer the requests of his children? The widow was persistent in asking, and we must be persistent in praying. This does not mean that we will always get what we pray for, but that God will answer us. We may ask for things that will do us more harm than good, so we must trust God to give us what we need.

Often we look at this widow and wonder whether we should keep asking God for the same thing. Some of us believe that we should take our burdens to the Lord and leave them. Those persons tell us that it is not necessary to remind God of our needs. Well, God does know what we need before we ask, but we need to pray. We need to verbalize our needs and believe that our requests will be granted. We need to pray persistently, but not just prayers of petition. We also must pray prayers of praise, adoration, confession, and thanksgiving. We can be squeaking wheels because God has the oil.

Lord, when you return, you will find me still praying. Amen.

A Burning Heart

Luke 24:13-35

They said to each other, "Were not our hearts burning within us while he was talking to us on the road, while he was opening the scriptures to us!" (Luke 24:32)

Have you ever had a burning heart? I don't mean heartburn, but a heart that is warmed by the power of the Word of God. When one's heart is warmed and burning with the power of the Word, that person must tell it.

This was the case with Jesus and the two who were walking to Emmaus. The two were talking about the death and resurrection of Jesus when Jesus, himself, joined them. They did not know it was Jesus, but they welcomed this traveler to journey with them to Emmaus. I can see them walking down that road, talking excitedly about the resurrection and not recognizing Jesus. They were anxious to share the news, for they could not believe that he was the only one in Jerusalem who did not know what had happened.

Jesus took over the conversation because he could see how reluctant they were to believe. He had to make it clear, so he started with Moses and the prophets and revealed to them all that had been written about him in the scriptures. I am sure their hearts started to burn during this conversation, but they may not have recognized the source of the burning because they did not know that it was Jesus.

The two must have been captivated by this stranger, for when they reached their destination, they invited him to stay with them and join them for supper. It was while Jesus was breaking bread that their eyes were opened, and then they had to go back to Jerusalem and tell it.

We may have a burning-heart experience when hearing the scriptures interpreted or in the breaking of bread for communion or in the pouring of water for baptism. It may even occur in the singing of a hymn. But whenever we recognize Jesus, our hearts will burn, and we must tell it.

Lord, I want my heart to burn with love as I tell others about the resurrection. Amen.

Come and See

John 4:11-30

Come and see a man who told me everything I have ever done! He cannot be the Messiah, can he? (John 4:29)

When I lived in Chicago, I often passed a church called Come and See Baptist Church. I was always amused when I saw the name, for I could just imagine inviting someone to visit the church and, when asked for its name, replying, "Come and See." Yet, that is the message of evangelism that the woman of Samaria proclaimed. She wanted all to come and see Jesus because he just might be the Messiah.

How often do we invite others to worship with us? Are we afraid to tell them to come and see? What will they see if they come? Will they discover

Jesus whom they will recognize as the Messiah, or will there be doubt?

Jesus took the time to talk with the woman of Samaria. He recognized her need for water. Oh, it was not the water that we normally drink. She needed the kind of water that would become a "spring of water gushing up to eternal life" (4:14*b*). But the woman did not understand. She knew that Jesus had no bucket and that the well was deep. Where would he get such water?

This is our question also. Where does Jesus get the water that gives eternal life? We need that water as much as the woman did.

Jesus was very clear. Before any of us can partake of that life-giving water, we must confess our sins and prepare to worship God in spirit and in truth. The woman confessed that she did not have a husband, and Jesus reminded her of the five she had had and of the adulterous situation she currently was in. Like that woman, we must evaluate our lives, past and present, before we can truly worship God and recognize Jesus as the Messiah.

We have been challenged to "come and see." Who is this Jesus? Can he be the Messiah? We can answer confidently once we have recognized that God is a spirit and that we must worship him in spirit and in truth. Come and see.

Holy Father, I confess my sins and seek to worship you in spirit and in truth. Amen.

THROWING STONES

JOHN 8:1-11

When they kept on questioning him, he straightened up and said to them, "Let anyone among you who is without sin be the first to throw a stone at her." (John 8:7)

❧

What would it be like today if we singled out all the men and women caught in adultery and gathered a crowd to throw stones at them? We might be able to catch lots of people guilty of the sin, but would there be anyone to throw the stones? I don't think so.

Jesus demonstrated the fact that all have sinned and fallen short of the glory of God by asking those without sin to be the first to throw a stone. Once this request was made, each person present had to evaluate his or her own life. Then, beginning with the elders, they dropped their stones and went away.

None of us is in the position to throw stones. Perhaps we all have not committed adultery, but we all have sinned. If we pick up stones, we are making judgments about the lives of others. Many Christians who have chosen a homosexual lifestyle accuse those of us who are heterosexual of throwing stones. They tell us that we judge them as sinners living outside the will of God. But all of us are sinners who often live outside the will of God.

The only time we know that Jesus wrote was while he waited for the first stone to be cast. What was he writing? Was he writing, "Sin is sin" or "Judge not lest ye be judged" or "Father, forgive them, for they know not what they do"? Any of these thoughts would have been appropriate, but all we know is that once all accusers had left, Jesus forgave the woman and charged her to go her way and sin no more.

Although we may not be caught in our sins or brought before a court or a crowd of accusers, we do not get away with sin. Eventually, we are held accountable. Jesus warns us to judge not and sin no more.

Holy Father, I drop the stones that I am tempted to throw. Amen.

NO ONE CAN TAKE YOUR JOY!

JOHN 16:16-24

When a woman is in labor, she has pain, because her hour has come. But when her child is born, she no longer remembers the anguish because of the joy of having brought a human being into the world. (John 16:21)

Jesus gives his disciples an example of the type of pain and sorrow that turns into joy. Having been in labor for twelve hours, I understand the childbirth illustration. As each pain hits, you wonder why you allowed yourself to get into such a painful situation. You just want it to be over. The amazing thing about my labor was that after so many hours, I had made little progress. So I had to have a cesarean section. But the joy of the child that was born took the pain away.

Evangelist Shirley Caesar sings a song with the

words, "This joy I have, the world didn't give it to me, and the world can't take it away." I felt that way about my child. No one could take away the joy I had experienced in giving birth. I understood that only God had developed that child in my womb and that no matter what, the world had nothing to do with it.

I also live the words of that song whenever I feel the presence of the Holy Spirit. When the Spirit moves within your heart, there is unspeakable joy. You know that God is alive and well in your life, and you realize the many blessings you enjoy. That is what Jesus communicated to his disciples. He was going away, and they would be sad for a little while. But when the Comforter, the Holy Spirit, came into their lives, they would know unspeakable joy.

The new joy, the unspeakable joy, that comes after the birth of a much-desired child or a heartfelt worship experience is accompanied by a peace that only God can give. One feels complete, fulfilled, and with that feeling is an opportunity to ask for even more blessings in the name of Jesus. When we experience that joy, we can ask anything of the Father in Jesus' name, and he will give it to us. No one can take away such joy!

Father, give me joy that is complete and internalized in my soul. Amen.

THE BIRTH OF THE CHURCH

ACTS 2

So those who welcomed his message were baptized, and that day about three thousand persons were added. (Acts 2:41)

❧

I can remember attending annual conference when I was a teenager. During the conference, each pastor reported the number of new members received during the year. Some ministers proudly announced that they had added one or two hundred members while others shamefully confessed that they had not added any. The presiding bishop asked pastors who had not added any or who had lost some of the ones they had why they had not worked harder. He told them that they should have gone into the neighborhoods and found people who were unchurched and convinced them to join. He was especially hard on those pastors whose family members had not joined. He always wanted to know what kind of pastor could not convince his family to become a part of his congregation.

My husband has been a pastor for thirty-six years, and he has never experienced a year when he did not increase the number of the church's members. He knew that he would get at least one new member, and that was me; and after our sons were born, he knew that he would get at least three.

But when Peter preached, three thousand were added. The church was officially born at Pentecost. Can't you just imagine the excitement? Everyone hears the message in his or her own tongue, and some are even speaking in unknown tongues. The Holy Spirit descends upon them, and they all are baptized. What a wonderful day that must have been!

What about our churches? Is there a need for a Day of Pentecost? Do our churches need to be reborn? Are they dead, or is the Holy Spirit moving in the pulpit, the choir, and the pews? Do you feel the spirit moving in your heart?

Lord, let your church be reborn, and let that rebirth begin with me. Amen.

A Helping Hand

ACTS 9:36-43

He gave her his hand and helped her up. Then calling the saints and widows, he showed her to be alive. (Acts 9:41)

❧

Dorcas is the only woman in the Bible specifically called a disciple. In fact, it is one of the first things said about her. I wonder how she earned that title. Well, it appeared that she was devoted to good works and acts of charity. Of course, that is what a disciple is supposed to do.

Dorcas became ill and died. In death, fellow disciples and saints surrounded her. Not wanting to believe that this kind, Christian woman was lost forever, they sent for help. They knew that Peter was close by, so they sent word for him to come without delay. Peter responded immediately.

Once Peter arrived, the widows took him to the place where they had laid her and showed him some of the beautiful clothing Dorcas had devotedly made for others. They told him all about her and why she was a disciple of the Lord. Peter asked them all to leave him alone with the body. Peter needed time alone to pray for the power to raise her from the dead. He humbled himself in prayer, kneeling before God. After praying and knowing that his prayers had been answered, he told Dorcas to get up.

Dorcas opened her eyes and saw Peter. She knew that he had told her to get up, so she did what she could without his help. She sat up. Realizing that she needed help to stand, Peter offered a helping hand.

Sometimes we need a helping hand. We may want to do what has been requested, but we can't do it by ourselves. Who will help us? Who will show the disciples of the church our good works and send for someone to offer a helping hand? Is it possible that we can offer a helping hand to someone in need?

Lord, help me recognize the times I need a helping hand and the times I can offer one. Amen.

I Am Not Ashamed

ROMANS 1:8-17

For I am not ashamed of the gospel; it is the power of God for salvation to everyone who has faith, to the Jew first and also to the Greek.
(Romans 1:16)

❧

What causes us to be ashamed? Do we experience shame because of external or internal forces? The dictionary defines ashamed as feeling shame, guilt, or disgrace or being kept back by pride. If we accept these definitions, shame may be the result of both external and internal forces. We may fear what others think of us or of our situation, or we may experience personal disgrace caused by our situation.

Paul was not ashamed of the gospel. It probably was difficult for him to make such a statement because he had persecuted those who had expounded the gospel before his conversion. But Paul had come to realize the power of God for salvation is for everyone who has faith, both Jew and Greek. He felt neither shame nor guilt because of his previous actions and beliefs, and pride did not keep him from accepting his own salvation.

Paul has set the example. Why are we ashamed? Are you ashamed? Let's see. Have you invited your neighbors and coworkers to church with you? Have you talked about the Bible study that you attend and greatly benefit from? Do you always insist on saying your blessing before meals even when you are eating in a restaurant? What if the people you are with do not want to say the blessing? Do you witness to them by saying your blessing anyway? Are you ashamed?

Some of us are ashamed that we do not know more about the Gospels and the faith that we profess. We dare not witness, for we fear being challenged and unable to defend our beliefs. What are we doing about that? Are we ashamed to admit that we do not know enough and have been reluctant to learn more?

We are challenged to profess our faith boldly, without shame or fear. It is powerful to be able to witness knowing that salvation is available to all who believe.

Lord, I will demonstrate today that I am not ashamed of the gospel. Amen.

Nothing Can Separate Us

Romans 8:31-38

Who will separate us from the love of Christ? Will hardship, or distress, or persecution, or famine, or nakedness, or peril, or sword? (Romans 8:35)

🍀

Only unbelief separates us from the love of Christ. When we reach that point in life when we feel that we no longer want to live, we are separated from the love of Christ. When we reach our existential breaking point and no longer want to go on, we are separated from the love of Christ. When we want to throw in the towel and just say "no" to life, we are separated from the love of Christ. Have you ever been there?

Paul makes it clear that none of the trials of life can separate us from the love of God in Christ. Consider Negro slaves as examples of those who suffered greatly but were not separated from God's love in Christ. They were brought to a foreign land, stripped of their freedom, made to learn new customs, a new language, and a new way of living, but they were not separated from the love of God in Christ. They composed beautiful songs that spoke of their connectedness to God in Christ.

There was a slave named Uncle Anthony who sang of his love for God in Christ every day. No matter how long he had to work in the fields for his master, he came home with a song on his lips. His wife would greet him, and they would sing together of the blessings God had granted them. When they were blessed with a child, they created even more beautiful, spiritual music.

Then one day Uncle Anthony's family was sold. He could no longer work in the fields; he just sang to God and asked that his family be provided for. A plantation owner felt sorry for him and bought his freedom. Uncle Anthony was last seen looking for his family and singing his own composition: "Nobody knows the trouble I see, nobody knows but Jesus; oh, nobody knows the trouble I see, glory Hallelujah!" Uncle Anthony was separated from his family but not from the love of God in Christ. Glory Hallelujah!

Lord, give me the wisdom to say "yes" to any of life's situations, knowing that nothing can separate me from your love. Amen.

Ready for Solid Food

1 Corinthians 3

I fed you with milk, not solid food, for you were not ready for solid food. Even now you are still not ready. (1 Corinthians 3:2)

There is much debate concerning the readiness of babies for solid food. Some doctors claim that babies should have nothing but breast milk for six months, while others want babies to have cereal at three months or less. There are so many different opinions that often mothers are left to their own discretion to determine when their babies are ready for solid food. I remember that my two babies were very different. While the older one might have been content with just breast milk for six months, the younger one wanted and needed more. I am sure that, like my two, each child is different, and the mother and doctor together must decide what the baby needs.

There was great division at the church at Corinth. Paul let them know that he came to them preaching Christ and Christ only. They were not ready to make decisions about their loyalties. While they were busy trying to determine whether they were followers of Paul or of Apollo, Paul wanted them to know that all had to be followers of Christ. They had to master the basics first. They were not ready for solid food.

So many of our churches today are like the church at Corinth. Some are followers of the pastors, while others are followers of the administrative board or the church council. Some groups within a church want to determine the church's mission and vision statement. Should that group be Christian Education or the Pastor-Parish Relations Committee? They have forgotten that Christ is the head; we all must be his disciples. We often forget to ask, "What would Jesus do?" We are not ready for solid food.

Until we are ready for solid food, let us enjoy the milk of learning and be Christ's disciples. Let us spend our time in studying the word and rejoicing in the spirit. And one day, we will be ready for solid food.

Lord, wherever I find division, help me bring unity under the precious name of Jesus. Amen.

PUTTING AN END TO CHILDISH WAYS

1 CORINTHIANS 13

When I was a child, I spoke like a child, I thought like a child, I reasoned like a child; when I became an adult, I put an end to childish ways.
(1 Corinthians 13:11)

Chapter 13 of 1 Corinthians often is read at weddings. It speaks of love and the qualities associated with it when that love is unconditional. In addition to being patient and kind, love bears, believes, hopes, and endures all things. And it never ends. This is the kind of love that all guests and the wedding couple hope they have.

Near the end of this love chapter, Paul writes of putting an end to childish ways. I always wonder whether the wedding couple thinks about putting an end to their childish ways. Their marriage would be in trouble if either partner decided to continue his or her childish ways. If one person always wanted his or her way or wanted to run home to Mama or Daddy, the marriage would be in trouble. What if either person continued to reason like a child, expecting Mama and Daddy to provide for his or her needs? What if either person refused to grow up? What if neither he nor she could accept the responsibilities of adulthood? If this happened, the marriage would be in trouble.

Paul lets us know that the unconditional love of which he wrote is possible only for adults. It is not childish, for unlike children, it is not selfish. It does not quit or run to divorce court at the first sign of difficulty. It is able to bear the loss of a child or the inability to have children. It continues when a partner is disabled and no longer able to care for himself or herself. It has put aside childish ways.

How does one find so mature and unconditional a love? Paul tells us that we must pursue love and seek to make it our aim, for love is greater than faith and greater than hope. It is not for children. It is only for those who have put an end to childish ways.

Lord, I want to have the mature, unconditional love that Paul describes. Help me learn to love maturely and unconditionally. Amen.

NOT MADE WITH HANDS

2 CORINTHIANS 4:16–5:10

For we know that if the earthly tent we live in is destroyed, we have a building from God, a house not made with hands, eternal in the heavens.
(2 Corinthians 5:1)

❦

Cancer can be such a devastating disease. If not detected early, it can destroy the body. Sometimes no matter what treatments are recommended and followed, the disease has too big a head start. The body cannot fight back. When all options have been exhausted, the patient may go to a hospice and wait for death.

I was blessed. My cancer was detected early in stage one. It had not spread to the lymph nodes and was confined to a small area of the breast. At the same time that I was diagnosed, a friend discovered that she also had breast cancer. She was not as fortunate. Her disease had spread to the brain, and her family watched the disease destroy her earthly tent. I am grateful that she was a Christian and that she had another building, one that was not made with hands.

It is so comforting for us as Christians to know that if the earthly tents we live in are destroyed, we have a building from God. This building is not made with hands, and it cannot be destroyed. It is eternal, and it is located in heaven. Even though our outer tents waste away, we do not lose heart. Our faith renews us day by day. We wait in anticipation of glory beyond all measure. What a wonderful promise of blessing!

Even without a devastating illness, our earthly tents waste away. As we age, we find that we cannot see as well, we cannot walk as well, and we may not be as alert as we once were. Our earthly tents are decaying. But what a blessing to know that there is a building not made with hands that will last forever. What a mighty God we serve!

Lord, thank you for the gift of spiritual bodies that are not subject to disease and decay. Help us be worthy to occupy those bodies eternally with you in heaven. Amen.

A Cheerful Giver

2 Corinthians 9:6-15

Each of you must give as you have made up your mind, not reluctantly or under compulsion, for God loves a cheerful giver. (2 Corinthians 9:7)

❧

There are so many reluctant givers. There are those who give at the office so their bosses will believe they are generous and interested in helping the company reach its goals. There are those who give so their names will be included in the church bulletin and others will admire them. There are those who give to get rid of the children who come to their doors asking for support of their schools and teams. I doubt that those who give under these circumstances ever receive a blessing.

My husband is one of the most generous people I know. I have to be careful about saying that I want something, for whether we can afford it or not, he will try to get it for me. He also extends this generosity to others. He says that every time he has given anything to anyone cheerfully, he has received a blessing. He claims that stingy people always struggle. They hold on to what they have so tightly that they cannot open their hands to receive their blessings. He is a prime example of one who sows bountifully and reaps bountifully.

What would it be like if we each decided to give cheerfully for one week? We would have to make up our minds to do it. We would have to reach into our pockets and willingly give. This means that we would give cheerfully to the building fund, the Boy Scouts, the schools, Little League, the United Way, and other funds. We would have to be willing to mail those letters to our neighbors and collect funds for the American Heart Association, cancer research, diabetes and kidney funds, and so on. Is that too much to ask? Probably. Most of us just don't have the resources to give to every cause, so we will have to give cheerfully to the causes that we believe in and that affect our lives. If everyone just did that, there would be funds in abundance. Are you sowing sparingly or bountifully? How cheerful a giver are you?

Lord, loosen my grip on my funds so that I may release them to help others. Amen.

What Does It Mean to Bear?

Galatians 6:1-10

Bear one another's burdens, and in this way you will fulfill the law of Christ. (Galatians 6:2)

Whenever I read this scripture, I remember a sermon I once heard on being a Christian to one who has suffered loss. The preacher used the letters of the word *bear* to outline his sermon.

For the letter *b*, he said, "Be there." When you hear that someone has suffered a loss, go to that person. You may not be able to do anything, but your presence will bring comfort. My husband followed this advice by stopping what he was doing to be with a young woman in our congregation who suffered a miscarriage. It is important to be there.

For the letter *e,* he said, "Encourage a discussion of the incident." Give the person who has suffered the loss an opportunity to talk. Your situation may not compare; so let that person tell you whatever he or she wants. Try not to make comparisons to what others have suffered. Each situation is unique.

For the letter *a,* he said, "Alter the situation." Once the person has had an opportunity to talk, change the subject. Help that person return to normal affairs. Life will and must go on. No matter how dark the night, there is joy in the morning.

For the letter *r,* he said, "Refer that person to the Master." Don't leave without telling about Jesus, the Author and Finisher of our faith. Those suffering loss need prayer. Pray with them, and let them know that you believe that God is able to heal their wounds.

Is there someone you need to be there for? Have you suffered a loss and need someone to be there for you? Perhaps the answer is yes to both questions. Be sensitive to those around you. Be that Christian friend for those who suffer, and you will find that there are many Christian friends available when you are suffering. The Golden Rule applies here.

Lord, I want to be there for others. Fortify me to bear their burdens. Amen.

EYES OF THE HEART

EPHESIANS 1:15-23

So that, with the eyes of your heart enlightened, you may know what is the hope to which he has called you, what are the riches of his glorious inheritance among the saints. (Ephesians 1:18)

❧

Does the heart have eyes? Can the heart see things that the eyes of the head cannot see? If I understand what Paul is writing, then the heart does have eyes, and those eyes can see. Once those eyes have been enlightened by the spirit of wisdom and revelation that comes from knowing God, they see what the eyes of the head cannot see. Those who do not know God see with only the outer eyes and judge things by physical standards. Those who have been enlightened judge by spiritual standards and can see what others cannot see.

Paul wanted the church at Ephesus to see with

enlightened eyes. He prayed that God would give them a spirit of wisdom and revelation so that the eyes of their hearts would be enlightened and they would know the hope to which God had called them. He wanted them to know the riches of God's glorious inheritance and the immeasurable greatness of his power to believers.

What a wonderful prayer! We need to join Paul in praying this prayer for all of our churches. Think about the blessings of church members who see with enlightened eyes. They would not be able to refuse pastors who were not of the race or gender that they expected. They would be able to see the pastor's vision and readily respond to the needs for mission in and around their community. They would know the hope to which God had called them. They would appreciate God's power and would have the gift of discerning God's will for their church and for their lives. They would know that Christ is the head of the Church and that God has put all power in his hands. They would know that the name of Jesus is above every name, not only in this age, but also in the age to come. The eyes of their hearts would be enlightened, and the blessings in store would be immeasurable.

Lord, enlighten the eyes of my heart with a spirit of wisdom and revelation as I grow in knowledge of you. Amen.

Easy with Love

Ephesians 5:21-33

*Husbands, love your wives, just as Christ loved
the church and gave himself up for her.
(Ephesians 5:25)*

❦

So many wives read verse 22 of the fifth chapter of Ephesians, "Wives, be subject to your husbands as you are to the Lord," and exclaim, "No way!" They consider themselves equal to their husbands and therefore should not be subject to them. They ask, "Why should the husband be in charge? Why is he the head of the family?"

I tell these wives to keep reading because when they get to verse 25, they no longer will be upset or fearful about being subject to their husbands. If they have husbands who truly love them, they know that their husbands will provide for them and do only what is best for them.

It is easy to be subject to one who loves you, for there is an element of trust that reigns. Confidence of the love that is shared leads to willingness to trust the judgment of the beloved. If a husband really loves his wife, he is willing to evaluate his competence in making the right decisions for the family. He may consult with his wife, but he knows that he is ultimately in charge and responsible.

Perhaps the divorce rate has reached an outrageous 50 percent because there is no head of the family. Everyone wants to be in charge. No one wants to be subject to anyone else. Neither partner experiences a love that bears, believes, hopes, and endures all things. If each marital partner is to remain independent and individually responsible, there is no need to marry.

Marriage is an agreement to love, care, provide, trust, and obey under the laws of God and society. If there is no leader in the marriage, it cannot function properly. It has no vision and no direction. It is easy to let a person who loves you be your leader.

Lord, give wives the willingness to be subject to husbands who love them and to refrain from marrying those who do not. Amen.

Pressing Toward the Goal

Philippians 3:7-21

I press on toward the goal for the prize of the heavenly call of God in Christ Jesus.
(Philippians 3:14)

❧

Goal setting is an interesting process. We must be able to conceive of the goal, and we must believe that we can achieve it. Then we must set a time limit. It is not a goal until we know when we have achieved it.

Paul had a goal of the prize of the heavenly call of God in Christ. He knew what that goal was; it was living so that he would eventually abide in heaven. He believed that he could achieve that goal and that other believers could achieve that goal. The time limit was earthly life. It was a lifelong goal that would be achieved at the conclusion of life on this earth. He would know that he had achieved it when he met God in Christ Jesus in heaven.

That is what I call a long-term goal. But if our lives are not long, then it may be a short-term goal. Whether it is a long- or short-term goal, we must press on toward that goal. How do we do that? Paul has some suggestions.

Paul tells us to forget the past. Suffering we have endured and accomplishments we have attained are not important. All that matters is that we make Christ our own. We must know Christ and the power of his resurrection and the sharing of his sufferings by becoming like him in his death. Many of us may decide to forget the goal of heaven because we do not want to share in Christ's sufferings and death.

Those of us still intent on achieving the heavenly goal are to be imitators of Christ. We are to give up the god of our bellies and take our minds off earthly things. We are to concentrate on pressing toward our goal, never believing that we have already attained it, but diligently moving toward it each day. Our citizenship is in heaven, and it is there that we are expecting to meet our Savior, Jesus Christ.

Lord, I'm pressing on the upward way. New heights I'm gaining every day. Still praying as I onward bound, just plant my feet on higher ground. Amen.

SONGS OF GRATITUDE

COLOSSIANS 3:12-17

Let the word of Christ dwell in you richly; teach and admonish one another in all wisdom; and with gratitude in your hearts sing psalms, hymns, and spiritual songs to God. (Colossians 3:16)

What kinds of songs do you like to hear and sing? I know that some people do not like secular songs at all; they listen only to religious music. But even in religious music, there are only certain types acceptable to them. They may listen to classical anthems or hymns based on the psalms, but spiritual and gospel songs are not for them.

I am glad that this scripture tells us that the word of Christ ought to dwell richly in us and that we ought to teach and admonish one another in all wisdom. When that is the case, we are not so picky about the types of songs that we hear and sing as long as they are sung with hearts of gratitude.

There are so many spiritual songs that were composed with hearts of gratitude. Consider "Plenty Good Room." The words include: "There's plenty good room in my Father's kingdom . . . Just choose your seat and sit down." Slaves were grateful that there was plenty of room in the kingdom that waited for them. All they had to do was be ready to occupy their place when the Lord called them home.

Then there are gospel songs composed with hearts of gratitude. Consider the old time gospel song "I'm So Grateful." Or perhaps the words to the contemporary gospel song "For Every Mountain" will speak to you of gratitude. This songs tells of God's many blessings and the praises that God is due. God has brought the composer over many mountains and through many trials, and for all of this, God deserves praise.

Whether we sing psalms, hymns, or spiritual songs, let us sing them with hearts of praise and gratitude, knowing that the word of Christ dwells within.

Lord, today, I will sing a new song. It is a song of thanksgiving. Amen.

FACE TO FACE

1 THESSALONIANS 3:6-13

Night and day we pray most earnestly that we may see you face to face and restore whatever is lacking in your faith. (1 Thessalonians 3:10)

No matter how many phone calls we make, letters we send, or e-mails we write, there is nothing like seeing and communicating face to face. When we can see the person we are speaking with, we can observe their body language, be warmed by their smiles, and rejoice in the feeling of their embrace. To be able to see a loved one face to face is worth praying for night and day.

Timothy brought Paul an encouraging report about the Thessalonians. He told of their faith and love and of their longing to see Paul. Paul let the

Thessalonians know how much their faith had sustained and encouraged him during his distress and persecution, and he thanked God for them and for the joy they brought him.

Even with this report from Timothy and the letter Paul sent to the Thessalonians, he still wanted to see them face to face. He wanted to see if there was anything he needed to do for them to strengthen their faith. He wanted to see that they were abounding in love for one another and that their hearts were being strengthened in holiness. He wanted to make sure that they would be blameless before God at the coming of Jesus.

Paul's motive for wanting to see the Thessalonians face to face was certainly a noble one. I wonder if we long to see our loved ones so that we can strengthen their faith or see if they are living in love and holiness. Are we praying for them night and day, or do we assume that they are living in such a way that they will be ready to meet Jesus? Meeting Jesus is the real face-to-face meeting, for which we all ought to prepare.

Lord, I want to see Jesus face to face. Help me to live so that one day I will. Amen.

ARE YOU A BUSYBODY?

2 THESSALONIANS 3:6-15

For we hear that some of you are living in idleness, mere busybodies, not doing any work.
(2 Thessalonians 3:11)

❧

I know several people who are so busy finding out what everyone else is doing that they do not accomplish anything themselves. They are what I call busybodies. They are busy doing everything but work. They make huge projects out of a few phone calls, for while they talk, they delve into areas about which they should have no concern. They may spend the day at the shopping mall visiting with other shoppers, or they may sit at the church and tell the secretaries and pastors what they ought to be doing. They are living in idleness and not doing any work.

Paul's second letter to the Thessalonians contains a warning against idleness. He tells them to stay away from believers who live in idleness. Those believers are not following the example that Silvanus, Timothy, and he had set. They worked night and day to pay for the food that they ate. Paul wrote, "For even when we were with you, we gave you this command: Anyone unwilling to work should not eat" (3:10).

I wonder how such a command would work today. Many people are in favor of restricting food stamps and other forms of welfare to those who are either working or being trained to work. Some people support day care centers in providing for welfare mothers so that they can work without being concerned for their children. These proposals may have merit, for I believe that people feel better about themselves when they earn their own money and make their purchases without restrictions.

Paul wanted everyone to earn his or her own living, and he challenged each one not to get tired of doing the right thing. He even told the Thessalonians not to have anything to do with those who did not obey his warnings. Paul believed that busybodies eventually would be ashamed. We don't want to join them.

Lord, keep me working productively every day of my life. Amen.

HAVE YOU DONE YOUR EXERCISES?

1 TIMOTHY 4:6-16

For, while physical training is of some value, godliness is valuable in every way, holding promise for both the present life and the life to come.
(1 Timothy 4:8)

❧

Doctors always recommend physical exercise. They tell us to walk, jog, dance, do yoga, and any other thing to increase our heart rate and help burn calories. We often resist this advice because we seem to be a nation of couch potatoes.

I have always had to watch my weight, so exercise is a part of my life. Three or four times a week, I do stretching exercises, followed by floor exercises, riding a stationary bike, and using the treadmill. Although these are all indoor activities, the important thing is that I do exercise.

❧

Even though my physical exercises are of some value to my health, Paul's first letter to Timothy warns that physical training is not enough. We need to exercise godliness, for it is valuable in every way and holds promise for both the present life and the life to come.

How do we exercise godliness? We must strive to be like God. Just as I have my three- or four-times-weekly physical routine, I need an everyday routine of godliness. My godliness routine includes praying, reading the Bible, researching and writing religious material, volunteering at the county hospital, teaching Bible study classes, conducting seminars, and participating in Christian worship. Although I do not do all of these things every day, I do some of them every day. I know that my participating in these activities makes my present life richer, and I hope they are preparing me for the life to come.

What is your godliness routine? Are you more faithful to your physical exercises than you are to your godliness or religious exercises? Neglecting your physical exercises can cause you to leave this present life prematurely, but neglecting your godliness activities can leave you with no life to come.

Lord, help me vigorously exercise my godliness every day. Amen.

GENERATIONS OF FAITH

2 TIMOTHY 1:1-14

I am reminded of your sincere faith, a faith that lived first in your grandmother Lois and your mother Eunice and now, I am sure, lives in you.
(2 Timothy 1:5)

❧

Timothy was blessed to have been a third-generation Christian. Both his grandmother and mother had sincere faith, and Paul was convinced that that faith had been passed on to Timothy. Reminding Timothy that he was benefiting from generations of faith must have been a source of encouragement, and it appears that Timothy needed to be encouraged.

Paul began his second letter to Timothy offering grace, mercy, and peace from God. He addressed Timothy as his beloved child and told him that he had been in constant prayer for Timothy. He recalled Timothy's tears but assured him that he had the type of faith that his ancestors had. Then Paul challenged Timothy to use that faith to stir up or rekindle the gift of God that was within him.

I am sure that Timothy had many gifts, but like so many of us, he was not using them. Paul told him to wake those gifts up, set a fire to them, and get them burning brightly so that others might see them and glorify God.

Perhaps we need someone like Paul to remind us of our home training. Many of us grew up in homes in which a mother or a grandmother prayed for us every day. Those women gave us strength and courage to face life, and they planted the seeds of faith within us. It is now time for us to rekindle our gifts and stir them up so that we can encourage others.

I have a friend whose mother was well known for her powerful prayers. After her mother died, my friend said that she had to stir up the gift of prayer within herself because someone had to keep praying for the family. Since her mother's death, she has become a powerful prayer warrior. She has benefited from generations of faith. She has rekindled her gift. What about you?

Lord, help me rekindle my gifts and encourage others to rekindle theirs. Amen.

WORTHLESS CONVERSATIONS

TITUS 1–3

But avoid stupid controversies, genealogies, dissensions, and quarrels about the law, for they are unprofitable and worthless. (Titus 3:9)

❧

Have you ever spent time, even hours, engaging in conversations that had neither purpose nor points of agreement? If you have, you were wasting your time. Those conversations were worthless. You probably have been warned not to discuss religion or politics because you might end up quarreling. You may have been warned never to talk about subjects that you are passionate about, for you may anger those who do not share your passion.

Paul advises Titus, his son in the faith whom he left in Crete to finish organizing the church, to tell the people to avoid stupid controversies. He knew that arguing about genealogies, points on which there could be no agreement, and points concerning the law served no purpose. Such conversations were unprofitable and worthless.

Paul wanted Titus to use his time wisely. Paul wanted him to appoint preachers in every town, preachers who lived righteous lives and knew the word. He wanted Titus to identify idle talkers who saw everything as corrupt. They were unbelievers who could not see what was pure because they were not pure. He wanted Titus to spend his time teaching sound doctrine, encouraging older men and women to be models for young men and women. He wanted Titus to be bold in the faith. There was no time for worthless conversations.

Paul ended his letter to Titus with a recap of what was expected of Christians. He told Titus to remind the people to be obedient, to do good deeds, to refrain from speaking evil, and to show every courtesy to one another. He told Titus to remind the church that they all had been saved by the grace and mercy of God through the water and the Holy Spirit. He also advised him not to have anything to do with those who caused divisions. There was no time for worthless controversies and conversations. There still isn't.

Lord, keep me from wasting time in worthless conversations. Amen.

Voluntary Acceptance

Philemon

But I preferred to do nothing without your consent, in order that your good deed might be voluntary and not something forced.
(Philemon 14)

※

$\mathcal{D}$o you remember times when your parents told you that you had to be nice to the new kid on the block? You did not like the looks of the new kid, and you did not understand why you had to share your toys or play with that kid. You liked to choose your own friends, but your parents forced you into acceptance.

Paul understood that no one likes to be forced into acceptance of another. So he decided to write a loving letter to Philemon and to those with him in the established church. He told them how close he and Onesimus had become. Onesimus was like his own child described as Paul's own heart.

Paul explained how useful Onesimus had become to his ministry and was sure that Onesimus would be useful to Philemon. Paul wanted neither to force Onesimus on Philemon nor Onesimus to be received as a slave. Paul asked that Onesimus be accepted voluntarily as a beloved brother. He even pleaded, "If he has wronged you in any way, or owes you anything, charge that to my account" (v. 18). Paul wanted there to be nothing standing in the way of Onesimus's total acceptance. So, confident that Philemon would do even more than he had asked, Paul felt that his heart would be refreshed in Christ through the benefit of this voluntary acceptance. He even told Philemon to prepare a guest room for him, as he expected to join them.

Forced acceptance is what many segregationist Americans fought. They did not want to accept slaves as brothers, but integration forced them. How wonderful it would have been if the Civil War could have been avoided and the slaves freed voluntarily. Forced acceptance of the freed slaves did not really work; the Civil Rights movement was necessary and perhaps still is more than one hundred years later.

Lord, give me a loving spirit that freely accepts others as brothers. Amen.

No Need for Sacrifice

Hebrews 10:1-18

Where there is forgiveness of these, there is no longer any offering for sin. (Hebrews 10:18)

❦

Sacrifice traditionally has been a part of religious rituals. Sometimes a sacrifice takes the form of a petition, a promise, or a gift. One may offer gifts in exchange for blessings. Or a sacrifice may be for the purpose of removing sin or pollution; it may even be an act of thanksgiving for blessings. But usually a sacrifice was offered for purification, or the removal of sin.

The writer of Hebrews recalled priests day after day offering the same sacrifices that could never take sins away. There was always a reminder of the sins year after year. The blood of bulls and goats could not wash away sin. But Christ, by the single sacrifice of himself, took away sin. God, through the sacrifice of his Son, covenanted to remember no longer the sins and lawlessness of those who believed and followed his commandments. There was no need for further sacrifice.

I wonder whether we still try to offer sacrifice for sin. When we have disobeyed God's commandments, do we offer a sacrificial gift? Do we promise to tithe faithfully for the rest of our lives? Do we volunteer to teach Sunday school or visit the sick? What sacrifice do we promise to make in order to be forgiven for our sins?

Hebrews lets us know that there is nothing we can do to remove sin. Our acts of sacrifice are no longer needed. God has accepted the sacrificial blood of Jesus, and it has washed our sins away. Our obligation in praise and thanksgiving is to live the way Jesus taught, to obey the commandments, and to refrain from future sin and lawlessness. We are saved by his grace, and nothing but the blood of Jesus can wash away our sins. There is no need for sacrifice. Thanks be to God!

Holy Father, thank you for the sacrifice of your Son and my Savior! Amen.

Nothing but Joy

James 1

*My brothers and sisters, whenever you face trials
of any kind, consider it nothing but joy.
(James 1:2)*

Some years ago, the United Methodist Women had the theme "Hallelujah Anyhow!" I love that theme because even when we face trials, we ought to praise the Lord. Our trials test our faith, and that testing produces endurance. Endurance helps us mature so that we are completely equipped to serve and obey the Lord through any circumstance. Our witness is that we find nothing but joy in our lives.

I wondered how three young couples in our church could count their recent trials as nothing but joy. Each couple was expecting their first child. The first couple gave birth to a premature stillborn son. He was fully developed externally but underdeveloped internally. The couple were devastated. They had prayed every night for a healthy baby, but their son was stillborn. How could they consider it nothing but joy? Somehow they did. They named and buried their son and looked forward to the next pregnancy. This trial left them stronger and more mature in their faith.

The second couple had great difficulty conceiving but at last they were successful. Although they thanked God everyday, at five months, the baby was stillborn. She was beautiful, but could not survive. The couple wondered why God had allowed them to lose their child. Hadn't they been faithful? They had to learn to count that trial as nothing but joy.

The third couple joyfully prepared for a baby shower. They were within a few weeks of delivery when the expectant mother developed a fever, and the baby died in the womb. They have rejoiced knowing that they can conceive.

These trials helped each couple grow in faith, develop endurance, and mature in the Lord. What trials have you endured? How mature is your faith? Do you count your trials as nothing but joy?

Lord, through each trial, help me say "Hallelujah Anyhow!" Amen.

Dead Faith

James 2:14-26

So faith by itself, if it has no works, is dead.
(James 2:17)

❧

$\mathcal{A}$nything dead needs to be buried, and anything alive needs to be active. I wonder how many of us have dead faith. We may claim faith and a belief in God, but we never do anything to demonstrate that faith. In other words, our faith is dead and needs to be buried.

In his letter, James asked, "What good is it, my brothers and sisters, if you say you have faith but do not have works? Can faith save you?" (2:14). Claiming faith and letting one's brother or sister exist without food or clothes was no good to anyone. We demonstrate our faith only by our works. If our faith is alive, it needs to be active in works.

One way I have chosen to demonstrate my faith is by volunteering at a hospital. I love children and I volunteer with children between the ages of twelve months and eighteen years. Most of the children I see are poor. Many of their parents are on welfare, and some of them do not know who their fathers are. This hospital situation affords many opportunities to support faith with works.

A mother was explaining to her daughter that she had to go to Las Vegas with her boyfriend. The child started to cry because it was her birthday, and her mother was not going to celebrate. The mother did not mention the birthday, did not bring any gifts, and did not ask the hospital staff to get her daughter a cake. She was eager to get on with her trip. The child was not important.

But I worked with the staff to get a cake and gifts for the child. We knew that it would not be enough to say, "Have a good birthday by yourself." We had to help a sick child understand that someone cared, someone who was willing to celebrate her birth. I knew that my faith was alive when I saw the smile that brightened that child's face when she saw the cake and the gifts.

Lord, help me keep my faith alive with works. Amen.

A Chosen Race

1 Peter 2:1-10

But you are a chosen race, a royal priesthood, a holy nation, God's own people, in order that you may proclaim the mighty acts of him who called you out of darkness into his marvelous light.
(1 Peter 2:9)

What does it mean to be chosen, and for what purpose has one been chosen? There are many times that we choose people; we choose people for jobs because of their qualifications and ability to do the work efficiently. We choose people for membership in organizations based on their character and contributions to their communities. We choose one particular person for marriage using criteria that may include personality, looks, intelligence, career goals, and so much more. We may even choose a place of worship based on the pastor and the members. We make many choices in life, and the reasons for those choices vary greatly.

God chose a race of people to obey his law and follow his commandments. He chose Abraham to be the father of that race, and he promised blessings for many generations. That chosen race often failed to be obedient to God's law and suffered punishment and exile to other lands. Every time God would send a prophet to redeem his chosen people, their acts of repentance were short lived. Sometimes they were obedient for a while, but they soon deserted their God.

But God had another plan. He decided to send his Son. Through the death of his Son, he redeemed his people, and they became a royal priesthood, a holy nation. They were again chosen, and this time they were chosen to proclaim God's mighty acts. God delivered them out of darkness into his marvelous light. These chosen people had to know that a mighty God had chosen them.

Peter charged these early Christians to live a holy life free from malice, guile, insincerity, envy, and slander. None of these characteristics qualified one to be a member of a chosen race, a royal priesthood. And they still don't. Do you want to claim your place as one of the chosen?

Lord, I want to be counted among the chosen race. Help me live a holy life. Amen.

God's Time

2 Peter 3:1-13

But do not ignore this one fact, beloved, that with the Lord one day is like a thousand years, and a thousand years are like one day. (2 Peter 3:8)

❧

We often make the error of confining God to our concepts of time and space. God's time is not like our time, and we cannot contain God in a box. God is bigger than both time and space. He is still in the past, with us in the present, and already in the future. A thousand years for us may be just a day for God.

This concept of God's time makes it easy to understand God's creating the world in six days. What was a day? Could it have been a thousand years? Would knowing how long a day was make a difference to those of us who were created by God? Could this knowledge be a way to merge evolution and creation? Think about it.

There are so many unanswered questions regarding God's time. We are eager to have our requests granted in our time. We, like children, want our way and want it right now. But God has his own schedule. God's time is not our time, and we must patiently wait for God to do whatever he wants when he wants.

A minister offered himself for the episcopacy. He felt that he was well qualified for the office of bishop, and he was eager to be elected. The election was held, and the minister was not elected. He was very disappointed, but he returned to his congregation with vigor and enthusiasm. During the next four-year period, he led his congregation in building a new sanctuary, increased its membership significantly, and provided much needed leadership in the community. When the next episcopal election was held, he was elected. His comment was, "I am glad that God's delay was not his denial." God acted in his own time. Wait on the Lord.

Lord, help me be willing to wait for your direction in my life. I submit to your will, your way, and most of all your time. Amen.

WALKING IN DARKNESS

1 JOHN 2:7-11

But whoever hates another believer is in the darkness, walks in the darkness, and does not know the way to go, because the darkness has brought on blindness. (1 John 2:11)

🌿

In his first letter, John writes to those he calls his little children that "God is light and in him there is no darkness at all" (1:5*b*). Those who claim fellowship with God must walk in his light. And by walking in that light, the blood of Jesus cleanses their sins. Those who walk in darkness can claim no fellowship with God.

What does it mean to walk in darkness? We walk in darkness when we disobey God's commandments, when we claim to be without sin, when we hate our brothers and sisters, and when we are out of the will of God.

There are so many examples of walking in darkness. Hating one another is a primary example. There are members of the Body of Christ, the Church, who hate each other. I have seen members who refuse to work on committees with certain other members. I have seen members who refuse to sit on the same pew with members of other races. I have seen members who refuse to accept their new pastor because he or she is not the one they really wanted. They all walk in darkness.

How can we move into the light? We must experience salvation. If we seek to become one with God and totally submit to his will, we will be saved. Our salvation is assured because we have an advocate with God, and that advocate is Jesus Christ who is the atoning sacrifice for our sins (2:2-3). Once we know the love of Jesus and share that love with our brothers and sisters, we have moved into the light.

There is no darkness in God, so why would we want to walk around without him? Walking in darkness is walking without light. We will bump into anything and everything. Turn on the light of God. Walk with him.

Lord, I need your light to guide me. I want to see where I am going. Amen.

Unwelcome Guests

2 John

Do not receive into the house or welcome anyone who comes to you and does not bring this teaching. (2 John 10)

❦

In John's second letter, he warns about those in the world who do not confess that Jesus Christ has come in the flesh. He tells his readers to be on guard so they will not lose the reward of knowing and believing in Jesus that they have worked so hard for. He instructs that those who do not abide in the teaching of Christ do not have God and should not be received into believers' homes. Welcoming such people is the same as participating in their evil deeds.

There will come a time when we will have to avoid welcoming certain people into our presence.

When we encounter those who are not believers and who deny the divinity and humanity of Jesus, we ought to try to convert them. We must be aware that whenever anyone professes a savior who is not of God, our association with that person implies our consent to his or her beliefs.

We often hear the saying "Birds of a feather stick together," the philosophy that John was reminding his readers of. Those who are not for Christ are not for God, and we do not need to stick together with them. They would not be welcome when we gather to pray and praise God for his many blessings.

As Christians, we are commanded to love one another as Christ loves us; therefore, we are compelled to witness to unbelievers. Witnessing is an easy task for those secure in the faith. Witnessing requires that we know Jesus Christ lived, died, and was raised from the dead. We must not let anyone destroy that belief and remain strong when we meet those who do not believe in the virgin birth or who accept only the humanity of Jesus, claiming that he was just another prophet like Moses or Muhammad. Such people are unwelcome guests.

Lord, give me the courage to witness to unbelievers and, as Jesus advised, to walk away from those who denounce my faith. Amen.

IS IT WELL WITH YOUR SOUL?

3 JOHN

Beloved, I pray that all may go well with you and that you may be in good health, just as it is well with your soul. (3 John 2)

❧

In his third letter, John writes to Gaius, one of his children in the faith. He has gotten a good report of Gaius's faithfulness and is commending him on that report. He prays that good health will be with Gaius as he flourishes in his faith.

What a wonderful testimony to John's ministry. Gaius is walking in the truth and showing hospitality and love to church members and strangers. John writes, "I have no greater joy than this, to hear that my children are walking in the truth" (v. 4).

John knows that it is well with Gaius's soul

because of Gaius's great faith. Is it well with our souls? Do we have great faith? Faith is required for our souls to be well.

A brilliant young man had a job that paid well and provided him the opportunity to use all of his talents. He was faithful in his church attendance, and his mother was so proud of him. She often relied on him to pray with her when she felt that it was not well with her soul. But the young man lost his job and fell into a deep depression. His mother was not as concerned about his losing the job as she was about what she perceived as his losing his faith. She wanted to know that no matter what happened, it was well with his soul. Like John, she wanted for her son not only good physical health but also good spiritual health.

As a mother, I often have prayed for the physical and spiritual health of my sons. I am convinced that their spiritual health affects their physical health. If it is well with their souls, they have the faith to overcome physical ailments. What an important lesson! Is it well with your soul?

Father, I am your child and I want you to be as proud of me as John was of Gaius. Keep me strong in the faith so that it will always be well with my soul. Amen.

Pray in the Holy Spirit

Jude

But you, beloved, build yourselves up on your most holy faith; pray in the Holy Spirit. (Jude 20)

❧

Jude's letter warns of worldly people who are devoid of the Spirit and cause divisions. He advises his readers to build themselves up on their most holy faith, to pray in the Holy Spirit, to remain in the love of God, and to look forward to the mercy of Jesus Christ that leads to eternal life.

I am intrigued by the admonition to pray in the Holy Spirit. The Holy Spirit is the third part of the Holy Trinity. How is the Holy Spirit involved in our prayers? We pray to God, the Father, through Jesus Christ, the Son, and with the Holy Spirit as our comforter and guide. Prayers offered in this manner are heard and answered. Their outcome depends on the will of God, but at least we are assured that they are offered in the right spirit.

A member of our church, Ed, suffered a stroke while he was at work. It is fortunate that he works at the county hospital, so he received immediate care. My husband was notified that Ed's prognosis was not good. With all the optimism expected of those who believe in answered prayer, my husband went to the hospital to see Ed. He knew that there was the possibility of permanent paralysis, slurred speech, and even a second stroke, but he laid hands on Ed, anointed him with the oil of the Lord, and asked for his full recovery. In other words, he prayed in the Holy Spirit.

Ed has fully recovered, and when he tells how his pastor asked God for his complete healing, he says, "He acted like he was asking for a pizza." Ed knew that his pastor was asking God to do a tremendous thing, but the pastor knew that it was a small thing for God. It was in fact no more than asking for a pizza.

Lord, when we pray in the Holy Spirit, knowing that you are all-powerful, and believing without doubt that whatever we ask in the name of Jesus will be granted, we have the assurance that you will answer our prayers. No task is too great for you to handle. Thank you. Amen.

The Beginning and the End

Revelation 1:1-8

"I am the Alpha and the Omega," says the Lord God, who is and who was and who is to come, the Almighty. (Revelation 1:8)

❧

As John prepares to write his words of prophecy to the seven churches in Asia, he makes sure that they understand who God is and what Jesus Christ has done for them. Their knowing that God has been with them from the beginning, through the present, and into the future is a good starting point.

Can anyone but God make such a statement to us? Our mothers were with us in the beginning of life, some of them are with us in the present, and others are gone. Our mothers cannot promise to be with us in the future. They do not know what the future will be. But God knows and has promised to be with us, not only in the beginning, but also at the end.

Knowing that God is almighty and that he will be with us no matter what happens ought to give us a feeling of peace. But does it? How many of us are not satisfied with the past, distressed and stressed in the present, and uncertain about the future? Do we forget that God has always and will always be with us?

Suzy had a loving mother. Her mother nurtured her from birth to the age of seven. Then her mother died of AIDS. Suzy was raised by her grandmother. Her mother had been with her in the beginning and wanted to be with her during the present and into the future, but it was not to be. It is fortunate that Suzy's grandmother taught her about God's love and dependability. She explained that it was important to know God and to remember that God is the Alpha and the Omega, the beginning and the end. Suzy soon will graduate from college. She has developed the musical talent God gave her and has prepared to teach others what she has learned. She has claimed her salvation and knows that God will never leave her. He is the Almighty who is, was, and is to come.

Thank you, Lord, for being the beginning and the end and all that lies between. Amen.